PRAISE FOR
CREATIVITY UNLEASHED

"This book made me cry, called me forth and lit a fire in me to CREATE more! Part anthem, part manifesto and part practical how-to -- this book will love you out of excuses and into making art that will change the world!"

> ~ *Sara Connell, bestselling author of* Bringing In Finn

"If you're looking to unpack whatever's stopping you from crossing the finish line on your creative projects, look no further. Part mindfulness journal, part adult coloring book, and part confessional from an accomplished artist who's courageously slain her own creative demons, with humor, heart, and tough love, Amber guides us step-by-step through the enchanting journey of manifesting our wildest dreams."

> ~ *Bianca Alexander, Esq., Executive Producer & Host,*
> Conscious Living *on PBS*

"If you take magic, enthusiasm, creativity, inspiration and put them all in a bottle and shake it up, then let it out--what do you get? One of the best books on Creativity ever written. It's fun, it's inspiring, it's educational, it's transformational."

> ~ *Charlene Tosi, Author of* Discover Your Woman Within,
> *and Founder of Woman Within International*

"With her wonderful wit, wisdom and wild ways, Amber invites us to put ourselves in the seat of power, to unleash our potential and fly! This IS the way to enjoy and complete the projects you long to bring to life!!"

> ~ *Shiloh Sophia, Curator, MUSEA :*
> *Center for Intentional Creativity®*

"Amber oozes creativity and authenticity and you can feel her soul in the pages of this book. Highly recommended for anyone looking to reconnect back to their true self through the power of creativity."

~ Natalie Southgate, Founder of Chakradance

"When Amber coaches creativity, she's truly coaching us to craft from ourselves the women we long to be."

~ Renee Tillotson, Founder of the Still & Moving Center

"Amber takes us on an inspiring and productive journey from 'Where do I start?' to 'Look what I did!' Whether you want to write your book, paint your masterpiece, or just feel ALIVE and FREE in your own skin, this book will serve as your trusted guide to an unparalleled creative nirvana."

~ Deborah Hurwitz, Founder and CEO of Cobalt Coaching

"Amber is 100% a present day GODDESS! *Creativity Unleashed* is a guide and invitation to women everywhere to make themselves (and their desires) a priority."

~ Lisa Marie Grantham, Women's Business & Empowerment Mentor, Founder of The Goddess Lifestyle Plan®

"Amber is brilliant at helping women unlock their sacred flow so they can get their creative projects done, release the barriers to self expression, fully step into their purpose and feel alive again!"

~ Wendy Collier, Founder of SoulFUEL®

"Anyone who desires to dig into their Pandora's Box of self-reflection through art will love this book."

~ Debbe Rosas, Founder Nia Technique, Inc.

"The journey you take within the pages of this book is one of pure liberation. Thank you for reading and marking this book up, making it your own. Our world needs full-color YOU right now!"

~ Whitney Freya, WhitneyFreya.com

"*Creativity Unleashed* is a gentle call to remind us of the importance of women's creativity and a loving companion to help guide us on the journey ahead!"

~ Cali White, Head of Partnerships at TreeSisters.org

"This book is the perfect way for any woman feeling stuck or uncertain to get started or back on track, and most importantly, moving and in flow."

~Karen Abend, Founder of Sketchbook Revival

"Thank you for writing a book that gives artists permission to be themselves and create!"

~ Heidi Easley, Artist and Founder at Texas Art & Soul

"Amber takes our hand and walks us across the bridge back to sanity, peace and creativity."

~ Anahita Joon, Founder of Beauty Unleashed
& leadership mentor to women

"Amber's work is filled with beauty, spirituality and optimism."

~ Tamara Laporte, Artist and Founder of Willowing Arts Ltd

"*Creativity Unleashed* isn't just just a book you read, it's a book you do to finally get those big ideas out of your head and into the world."

~ Elizabeth Foley, Artist, Radiant Art Studios

"In this gorgeous book, Amber Kuileimailani Bonnici, the reigning goddess of sublime creative expression, will show you how to connect to the wonder, magic, and life-transforming energy that's already inside of you. Just show up with an open heart and let your renaissance begin."

~ Cynthia Occelli, Mentor, Mother,
bestselling author of Resurrecting Venus

"Amber invites creativity to be a sacred and simple way of everyday life."

~ Sacha Sterling, Founder of Thrive Virtual

"I love the energy of the book! This is for anyone looking for a new way to heal, inviting you to explore the depths of your innermost soul."

~ Louis Reed, Founder of Energy Medicine Institute

"*Creativity Unleashed* offers a Divine roadmap back to your Creative Spirit."

~ Alexis Cohen, Visionary Artist and
Founder of Art Medicine LLC

SISTERHOOD

Sometimes when you do this kind of work, things come up. If choosing to create and finally do that thing you've been called to do feels scary, overwhelming, or big, know you don't need to do this alone. We are doing it. Together.

As a Creativity Unleashed sister, we'd like to gift you 1 ticket to one of our upcoming online retreats to get you into creative momentum. Imagine awakening your creative spirit, learning your creative cycle, and getting into creative flow while creating with others.

Go to **www.womanunleashed.com/unlockflow** to claim your ticket today.

Creativity
UNLEASHED

A WOMAN'S GUIDE TO UNLOCK FLOW AND
FINALLY FINISH CREATIVE PROJECTS EVERY DAY

AMBER KUILEIMAILANI BONNICI

**Compassionate Mind
Collaborative**
cmcollab.com

Illustrated by Amber Kuileimailani Bonnici.
Edited by Heather Doyle Fraser.
Designed by V BELL DESIGN.
Proofed by April Kelly.

ISBN: 978-1-7372006-2-8

For my LOVE, Tony,
who has taught me
partnership can amplify our gifts

&

my boys Sage and Bodhi,
who have taught me
there is always more love to give.

CONTENTS

Top Creativity Blocks
+ THE PATH FORWARD 211

Revisit for CREATIVE MOMENTUM 263

Introduction

The time for women is now.
To do your creative work.
To unleash your gifts into the world.
To share yourself, all of yourself with others.

There are women who are sitting on ideas that will change our world. Sitting on them because they don't think they are smart or fabulous or amazing enough to share them. Sitting on them because they are afraid of what others will think. Sitting on them because they are taking care of others and feel guilty about spending time on their ideas or visions.

Maybe that's you?

If we were sitting down over a cup of tea, I'd tell you, your time is now. Don't wait.

There are painters not painting.
Writers not writing.
Dancers not dancing.
Teachers not teaching.
Photographers not taking photos.
Entrepreneurs not starting businesses.
The world is full of people not living.

When you aren't living, life often looks more like an endless to-do list, filled with things you are taking care of for other people. But what about you?

Most of my beloved clients are in midlife. They've taken care of others, their kids, their careers, and they finally wake up one day and say, "Enough. I need to do that thing I always wanted to do."

This book is my gift to you. One that will help you take that idea, maybe one you've kept secret and always longed to manifest, and finally DO something about it.

My hope with this book is for you to take those half-finished, half-baked ideas and finish them. I want you to bring your creative gifts into the world. Because there is NO ONE else in the world who will create what you will the way you will. And if you don't do it, no one else will.

There is a vitality,
a life force, an energy,
a quickening that is
translated through you into
action, and because there is
only one of you in all time,
this expression is unique.
And if you block it,
it will never exist through
any other medium
and will be lost.

– MARTHA GRAHAM

In short, this book is for you if you...

Feel like you've lost your creativity (or don't even know if you have any).

Have always had a dream to _____ (write a book, show your art in a gallery, teach a workshop, start a business, fill in the blank), but never got around to it.

Can't seem to focus enough to get anything done.

Start things but have trouble finishing them.

Have Shiny Object Syndrome and jump from idea to idea.

You're not doing what you really want to be doing and are ready to change that.

HOW TO USE THIS BOOK

This book is part guidebook, part journal... Think of it as one part inspiration and instruction, one part get it done.
Bend the pages.
Write all over.
Color sections.
Paste magazine images in.
Add glitter if you'd like.

Let this be your book. Use her up.

There is SO MUCH information out there. Sometimes when I'm learning something new, I feel full. Like I ate too much at Thanksgiving dinner. Stuffed.

Your head is like that. Stuffed.

It's time to take that information, those ideas, and DO something with them. To not only use your head knowledge, but to also bring it into your body, to bring it into the experience. That is where wisdom comes. It's this place after knowing. It's in the DOING.

This book will get you DOING.

You're done thinking about it,
Visioning,
Praying,
Meditating,
Talking about it.

You're gonna do it. Let's get started...

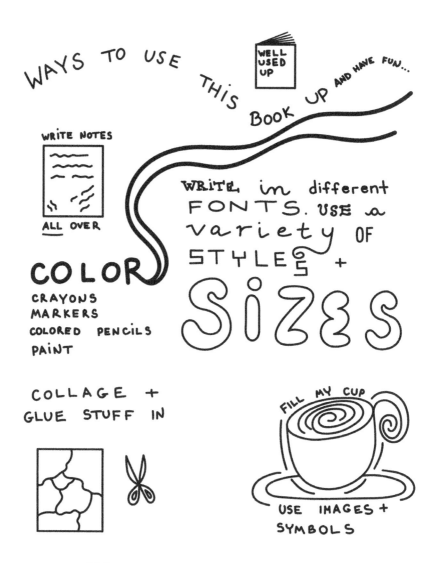

WAYS TO USE THIS BOOK UP AND HAVE FUN...

WELL USED UP

WRITE NOTES ALL OVER

WRITE in different FONTS. USE a variety OF STYLES + SiZES

COLOR
CRAYONS
MARKERS
COLORED PENCILS
PAINT

COLLAGE + GLUE STUFF IN

FILL MY CUP

USE IMAGES + SYMBOLS

MAKE THESE PAGES LiVE. GET MESSY.

HAVING FUN IN THE BOOK

You've got two sides of your brain. Most of the time, we just use one of those sides. We're taking information in and filing it, based on our past experience. Most of us are hanging out in the left side of the brain. Do. Do. Do. We're going to open up and use that other side of the brain. Extra power.

By doing CREATIVE note-taking, we're able to access BOTH sides of the brain. We're opening up more receptors, being able to see and open to more possibilities, more energy, more power.

Here are a couple of ways to take notes CREATIVELY, open up the right side of your brain, and have fun while reading this book:

WRITE NOTES
In the margins, in sections labeled notes, wherever you want.

WRITE IN DIFFERENT WRITING STYLES
Block print, script, cursive. Add dots, lines. Make your first letter big and then the others small. Mix it up.

WRITE IN DIFFERENT SIZES
Play with the size of the writing. Use big writing for important things and small writing for things that aren't as important.

COLOR
Crayons, markers, colored pencils. Use them. Different colors for different ideas. Red, blue, green, magenta, grey. As your ideas grow, this book will too, from black and white to color.

SYMBOL AND IMAGE
If I'm speaking of a metaphor or an image comes to mind, draw it in. If I'm talking about filling your cup and taking care of yourself, draw a cup and write on the side, "Fill My Cup." Doodling welcome.

COLLAGE

Flip through a magazine and grab some images and words. Add them to this book. Let your book get thick. Extra points if you need a rubber band to hold it together.

You WANT this book to feel used. Very used.

What's cool about this way of note-taking is first, your brain takes so much more in. It remembers more, thinks of connections, ideas, inspiration. Your brain fires differently. And, as a bonus, when you flip through the book, it's easier to find things, sections, ideas you want to implement.

For now, let's get you comfortable messing up this book (gasp!). In the space below either write, draw, color, or collage something here...

After, take a pic and share on social media. Use the hashtag *#creativityunleashed*

CHANNEL OF LOVE

CHAPTER 1

Creativity
UNLEASHED

You are born to create. You're made for it. Created after the Creator. It's in your DNA. In your bones and blood. It sings to you late at night or in the quiet spaces between spaces.

When you don't create, things go wrong.
Depression,
Anxiety,
Dissatisfaction,
A sense that something is off.
It is.
You're not creating.

When you bury and stuff your creation energy, it still bubbles. It still yearns to come out. Only sometimes it doesn't fit in your plan. It doesn't make sense. It's in a different category than making a living or reducing world hunger or being productive.

Everyone has a creative calling.

It doesn't matter how big or small, significant or not. Whether you are creating a book, Ph.D., painting, business, piece of music, or garden it doesn't matter. Creative callings often don't make sense in the traditional sense, but they satisfy something deep within. They are a part of your spirit.

They feed a hunger. The hunger to make a mark.

Because that is the point of creativity... YOU making an impact, a lasting impression, letting others experience the totally unique, totally you side of you. Creation is powerful.

It is taking things from the unseen world and making them seen. An idea, a thought, a vision, and bringing it to the physical world. You're a midwife of dreams and ideas, a gateway between imagination and reality.

This book was an idea before you could read it.
That painting was an idea before you could see it.
That garden was an idea before you could walk through it.
That business was an idea before it was working.
That workshop was an idea before you taught it.
That Ph.D. was an idea before you went through school.
That house was an idea before it was built.
That chair was an idea before it was designed.
That hairbrush was an idea before it was created.
That necklace, dress, shoe, car, meal... all ideas, thoughts, dreams.

And yet, I hear people tell me all the time...
I'm not creative.

Wrong.
You are.

Ninety-five percent of 2nd graders believe they're creative.
When they enter 5th grade, only 50% believe.
In high school, only 5%.

If you believe you aren't creative, it's just because creativity has been trained out of you. Trained out because it doesn't fit in.

Let that sink in.

MY CREATIVE PATH

In elementary school, I dreamed of being an author. I wrote and illustrated my stories. Nancy Drew meets Black Beauty. It made me so happy to come up with these adventures.

One day I brought my most recent story to my teacher. She looked at it, smiled, and said, "Artists and Writers don't make a good living. It's a really hard path. You have to be really good to do that."

I knew she meant I wasn't good enough. I started comparing my drawings to other kids in my class and realized mine didn't look as good. My horses didn't look realistic. My ladies' heads were too big.

I believed her. I decided I wasn't an artist.
I stopped creating for 20 years.

When it came time for me to decide on my first elective class I chose band instead of art. I played the trumpet, then the french horn for six years. I learned to play the piano and a little guitar. I knew I had a gift as a musician, especially if I worked hard and practiced.

I told myself I wasn't an artist through high school when drawing elaborate posters for my English class project. I told myself I wasn't an artist during my exchange year in Finland even when my drawing was selected as a cover for the school yearbook. I told myself I wasn't an artist in college when I designed a program with music and graphics.

You see, if I told myself I wasn't an artist, I wouldn't be disappointed. When that critic came around, because she always did, telling me my work or writing or art or drawings or graphics weren't good, I could agree with her. I wasn't an artist.

Art was something you were gifted at. I didn't believe it could be within me already, that I was already a creator.

I did art on vacation, during playtime. I could collage and draw and write and it didn't matter, because I wasn't an artist. I was only doing it for fun, dabbling.

I took a job that made money, the corporate path. High-tech marketing for a while then retail management where I managed a seven-figure business. I would work 60- to 80-hour work weeks, I was good at what I did. Work was my life (as my husband would point out to me). When I went on vacation, I would completely unplug and go to my family's home on the Northern coast of California.

One day I was walking through town, window shopping, and I saw a space I'd never seen before.

The store contained artwork, paintings, images of women by an artist, Shiloh Sophia. Each piece seemed to talk to me. I walked out of the store with a Coloring Journal filled with feminine images and I started coloring and drawing, collaging and journaling. That book became my container for dreaming.

Around that time I decided I wanted to be a mom.

We became pregnant. I was ecstatic. I thought I'd keep working and Tony, my husband, would watch the baby. We would stay up late at night planning, reading about babies, so, clearly, we were gonna be the perfect parents.

I was on a business trip and woke up in the middle of the night cramping. I thought, Oh God, no. I got up quietly so I wouldn't wake the other woman staying in my room and went to the bathroom where I saw I was spotting. I called my doctor and she confirmed I was losing my baby. I called Tony so scared.

He was a state away and couldn't do anything but listen to me cry. When I finally made it back home I had to deal with going to the doctor, knowing I wasn't going to hear the heartbeat anymore. Hearing from friends and family, "You'll have another baby. There is a reason for everything." All I knew was that it hurt a place so deep within me I couldn't name it.

So I did what I normally did when the pain was too much. I got busy.

I went back to work the next day to take my mind off my baby. As I was working, one of the other managers came in to check on my store. She was one of the few who knew what had happened. She was shocked to see me and asked what I was doing there. I said I had work to do and needed to be there.

What she said to me next, I'll never forget.

She said, "You'll always have work. You HAVE to make a choice about what is most important to you. Take care of you so you can have a family."

So I went home. I stayed in bed in my pajamas with the shades drawn for three days. I didn't eat. I just slept and cried. Tony didn't know what to do. At one point he even asked me, "Are you sure you were pregnant?"

I felt utterly alone.

When I finally did crawl out of that dark place I started asking myself what I really wanted.

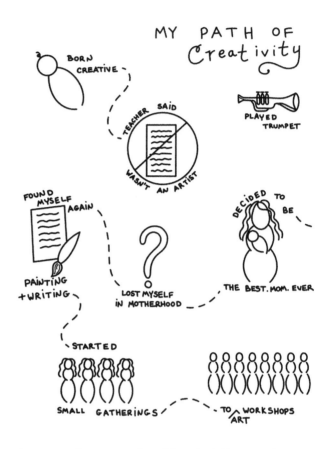

What was it that I wanted my life to look like? I made a commitment. I would put my family first.

Tony and I became pregnant again. I was going to be the best. Mom. Ever. I read all the right books. I knew the latest research on what to do and not do with babies. I read about birth and sleep training. I watched other moms.

When Sage was born, I felt a love I had never felt before. I decided then not to return to work. Instead, I dedicated myself to him. All of the energy that I had put towards my career poured into my child and my family.

So, for the first time in my life I not only entertained the idea of staying home, I became a stay-at-home mom. During that time, Tony and I decided to move and we had another baby. Tony was now working extra hard to pay for two houses. He traveled for three months and came home for 10 days. Gone then home. Again and again on repeat.

So my life became very narrow -- it was me and a two-year-old and a baby for company. Sleepless nights. Baby crying. My whole day revolved around meals, diapers, and nap time. I tried to get out and see people, but just to take my kids to the local library for storytime was a two-hour experience.

Once we got there, I was chasing after my oldest as he'd pull books off the shelves.

I remember thinking, *Is this what my life is? Where have I gone?*

I found I had darker and darker thoughts. I would stay in bed all day unless the baby was crying or Sage was telling me he was hungry. I just wanted it to end. At one point when I was bathing my baby and he was crying, I thought about sticking him underwater, how everything would finally be quiet. In that moment, I knew something was wrong. I needed help.

I started talking to my in-laws. They took the boys on days when everything got to be too much.

I started reading to pull me out of that dark place. One book I read was called, *The Gift of a Year*, by Mira Kirshenbaum. The author invites you to choose one thing to focus on for the year, One thing that makes you happy. I went through the exercises in the book and looked for things, ANYTHING that would light me up again. And I remembered those stories I used to write when I was a kid... writing and painting. What would life be like if I did that again?

I prayed.

The very next day an email popped in my inbox inviting me to a six-month online painting and writing course, LEGEND, by artist Shiloh Sophia. I knew it was Spirit answering my prayer.

So I took my Christmas and Birthday money and decided to do something totally for me. I signed up for that six-month mentorship. I had SO many other things that money could have gone towards. My kids, our bills, our house, food. I had to battle that voice in my head saying I was being selfish.

I felt guilt.

I was so desperate, though, I didn't care.

I chose myself.
Not my kids.
Not the house.
Not my husband.
Me.

I miraculously figured out how to get both boys to take naps at the same time. SACRED NAP TIME. I would paint during that 30- to 60-minute block. I let the dishes pile up. I let the house be messy. I was single-minded, single-focused.

Once I got into the routine of nap time creativity time, I started waking up early, before the kids. I would go for a morning walk before the sun rose or go to a café and write.

I had these blocks of time I lived for. These were the times I felt alive, times when I remembered who I was. Times where I let creativity flow, and I let myself have fun. And bit by bit, I started my journey back home to myself.

I recognized my desires again.
I started to dream.
I felt hope.
I had something to look forward to again.

Choosing me, choosing creativity, brought me out of my depression. Creativity led me out of the darkness. She reminded me of the light.

Now draw your own CREATIVE PATH...

RECLAIMING YOUR PIECES

She reminded me of my calling.
And I listened.

I discovered pieces of me I had buried.
Leashed. Set aside when they didn't
fit in. I found something bigger than
my waking days as a mom. I found me.

And so I started my reclamation.
As an artist, a writer, and a visionary.
My artwork started selling.
My writings published.

When I had enough energy to do more
than care for myself, I heard creativity
calling me to share with others. When
I had healed enough, I wanted to help others do the same.

That's what we're really talking about here, reclaiming a piece of
you. The pieces you've sacrificed on the journey to fit in. Your
creativity, your voice, your uniqueness. The pieces that were too
loud, too big, too much.

There is an awakening, a remembering. You've realized you
don't want to sacrifice those pieces. You're ready to unleash
your creative power.

It's time.

YOU
ARE
WORTH
IT

DESIRE

It starts with desire and choice.
First, you have to know what you want.
Next, you have to choose it.

In order to choose, you have to know what you want. And if you don't know and haven't spent time asking yourself what you want, you'll do things based on what OTHERS want.

It took practice for me to know what I wanted.
I started small.
What I wanted for dinner.
What I wanted to wear.
What color nail polish.

I practiced giving myself permission to want.
Permission to want for me.
Just me.

So as the Spice Girls say,
"Tell me whatcha want, whatcha really, really want."

Let's start with exploring your way of being.
How do you want to BE?
How do you want to FEEL?

Write what comes up right now...

Sometimes, when you are just starting out, it's hard to remember how you want to feel. So, here are some ideas for how you may want to feel, just to get you started...

Happy
Joyful
Connected ·
Loved
Loving ·
Passionate
Creative
Driven ·
Ambitious
Focused ·
Inspired
Free
Awesome ·
Playful
Peaceful ·
Trusting
Positive
Balanced ·
Harmonious
Powerful ·
Authentic
Giving ·
Generous
Truthful
Alive ·
Appreciated
Grateful ·
Satisfied
Open ·
Confident
Accepting
Calm ·
Curious
Determined ·
Secure
Certain
Bold ·
Brave
Daring ·
Energetic
Serene ·

CHOICE

You are now at choice.

The things you want don't just happen. If you are not choosing for yourself, then someone or something else is choosing for you. That's when life happens to you and you wake up years later wondering how you got where you are.

It's easy not to choose.
Letting others choose for you means you don't need to be responsible. You don't have to think too much.

Letting someone else choose to handle your money, bills, and taxes,
Letting your boss choose your time on or off,
Letting your partner choose how you spend your household money,
Letting your kids choose,
Letting your parents choose,
Letting your friends choose,
Letting your family choose,
Being swept up by the choices that everyone else makes.

Letting others choose for you is a choice.

I'm here to remind you, choose YOU.
Choose your creativity.
Choose your passions.
Choose your dreams.
Choose your calling.

Choose.

Unless you choose you, things won't change.

Eight years ago my life changed when I chose to do something just for me. Painting & Writing. That one choice was a catapult for everything else. I started taking care of my health. I started doing small workshops, teaching, hanging work in galleries. I started an online business, built a team, founded the Woman Unleashed Movement. Choice after choice.

It started with one. One choice at a time. What do you choose?

What do you choose to believe about yourself? Are you doing good or failing? Is what you're doing enough or never enough? Think about it.

. . . .

. . . .

. . . .

. . . .

. . . .

. . . .

. . . .

. . . .

What do you choose to believe about creativity? Is it important? A waste of time? Good for work but not for play?

. . . .

. . . .

. . . .

. . . .

. . . .

. . . .

What do you choose to do with your time? Or better question, what do you choose NOT to do that you really want to?

. . . .

. . . .

. . . .

. . . .

. . . .

. . . .

WHY DO YOU LOVE TO CREATE?

One of my favorite reasons to create is it makes me feel connected to Spirit. When I'm writing a story and I'm in flow, I feel on purpose. When I'm painting and allowing Spirit to move through me, I feel happy and free. When I dance, I feel peaceful.

Why is creativity important to you?

. . . .

. . . .

. . . .

. . . .

. . . .

How does doing your creativity make you feel?

. . . .

. . . .

. . . .

. . . .

. . . .

What are you letting others choose for you?

CALLING CHOICE POINT

Some women feel the calling and they jump in with a 100% yes. Others feel the calling, are scared, terrified even, and still jump in. Others feel the calling, but something stops them.

You want to change careers OR
Write the book OR
Start teaching creativity classes online OR
Begin a woman's circle OR
Build the retreat sanctuary but...

You're NOT SURE.
You're SCARED.
You haven't followed through before so you've LOST your self-trust.
You CAN'T SEE how it will work.
You can't JUSTIFY (the money or time) in your mind.
And so you stop.

You've hit the Calling Choice Point.
And that moment pushes ALL your buttons because your calling is your spiritual path.

Each of my Calling Choice Points pushed me way out of my comfort zone.

When I chose to take my first painting/writing class my mind told me it was a waste of money, I wasn't an artist and I didn't know what I was doing, but I felt the calling and did it anyway.

When I chose to hold my first woman's circle, my mind told me I had nothing to share, no one would come, I'd look like a fool, but I felt the calling and did it anyway.

I didn't have experience.

I didn't have money.
I didn't have time.
I didn't have proof it would work.
I had to step out in FAITH.

You need faith to do something you haven't done before.
You don't know what's going to happen.

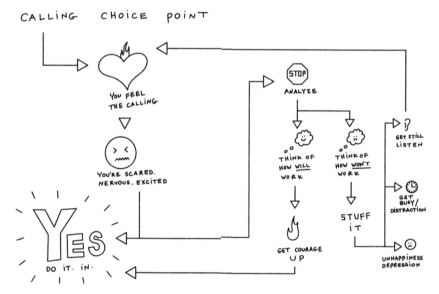

So if you are in a Calling Choice Point, remember Callings aren't safe. They don't make sense to your mind or to others when you try and explain them. There is no proof they'll work. And that is why most people just sit on their callings or stop just short. Because they're not sure.

But there is a cost to ignoring it...
Depression. Isolation.
Disconnection from your spirit.
A feeling something is wrong.

Sister, whatever calling YOU are feeling now, remember you have a choice. You have to CHOOSE your calling. What do you need to do to choose it?

. . . .

. . . .

. . . .

. . . .

. . . .

. . . .

. . . .

. . . .

. . . .

. . . .

. . . .

. . . .

Remember, your calling is a spiritual journey. Faith is required. And there is freedom on the other side.

PRESENCE

As creative women, it's easy to get overwhelmed. We have loads of ideas and then even more ideas about how to do the ideas. We're pulled in different directions.

I get asked all the time, "How can you be a mom, run a business, have a husband, workout, travel, visit friends and family...? The answer... Being present.

PAST   PRESENT   FUTURE

3 BREATHS

If you get overwhelmed easily,
If you can't get clear,
If your energy feels scattered,
If you have lots of different focuses but aren't getting movement,
It's time to tap into the Power of Presence.

Your power isn't in the past. It isn't in the future. It is here. Now. You create now.
Take action now.

Presence takes your energy that is focused on lots of different areas and projects and allows you to focus in one direction. It takes scattered energy and laser-focuses it. It also helps you focus on the one thing that is right in front of you. Everything becomes so much less overwhelming because all you have to do is focus on the one thing in front of you.

Presence creates connection. With your work, with others, with Spirit.

Every single time I begin a session, whether it's a workshop or teaching with our Unleashers, we take three breaths together. It's a way to get open and receptive.

Open to what you need to hear.
Open to what you need to see.
Open to what you need to feel, and
To Know.

When doing your creative project, I'm going to invite you, if you have other stuff going on, to shut it down, to get really present.

Take a moment and notice anything that's on your mind from before this moment, any energy or emotion or thoughts that are pulling you from before this moment. Take a deep inhale and exhale.
Let that go.

Next, notice if there's anything coming up that's on your mind. You may be thinking about this book or an upcoming project or what you're having for dinner, something that's happening later today that's pulling you from this moment. Let's inhale in and exhale.
Let that go.

Our third and final breath, inhale and smell this moment, this time. There is nowhere else to be, nothing else to do. Be here now. Smell the moment and exhale.

Now we're ready to jump in.

INTENTION

Intention is about desire. Will. Choice. Without intention, you react. Setting an intention is like a boat putting down an anchor. You're going to stay in the general area, no matter what's going on with the waves.

Intention takes your energy and moves it in one direction. Like presence, it takes scattered energy and focuses it.

My second mom, Viv, taught me the power of intention. She was visiting from the mainland. My husband and Dad were off on a men's weekend and we were going to have some girl time. She thought she'd help me clean the house and take care of the kids. As we were talking the first day, she said, "Let's set an intention. What do you want from our time together?"

My intention was connection and rest. Her intention was creativity and love.

Shortly after we set our intentions, we were invited to a party. Filled with my friends and a local band, it was sure to be fun. Shortly after talking it through, we realized it wouldn't fit our intentions. It wasn't going to give us the connection and love we wanted with one another since we'd be with others. We said no.

The next morning we woke up ready to start cleaning the house. Then we realized that wasn't going to give us rest and creativity. We decided instead to hire a local teenager to come over, tidy up the house, and watch the kids. Viv and I went into my art studio and painted.

We created connection, rest, creativity, and love.

What we created wouldn't have happened if we hadn't set our intentions. We would have gone to the party and cleaned the house.

Intention helps you make aligned decisions.
It helps you get clear.
It helps you direct your energy and focus.

YOUR CREATIVE CALLING

This is where you can dream, that secret place in your heart, that space you think -- *Oh I'd really like to* _____ *someday.*

Maybe you're already doing it. Maybe you're still thinking about it or figuring it out. It could be anything from painting or drawing to writing a book, or teaching a workshop or class. It could be anything.

Write it down here. Write as if this one thing you're dreaming might happen someday is happening right now. In present tense, write as much detail as you can come up with. Already done.

Here's a little example to get you thinking: *I am sitting down in a bookstore. There is a line of people waiting to sign my book. A woman comes up and says... This book got me to finally finish my painting series.*

If you're creative, of course you have loads of ideas. That's why I've given you lots of space. You're welcome!

JEWELRY MAKING

COOKING + CUISINE

PAINT A PAINTING AND SHARE WITH OTHERS

PLAYING MUSIC . SINGING

WHAT'S YOUR Creative CALLING ?

GARDENING

WRITE A BOOK. POETRY . BLOG

LEAD A WORKSHOP

INTERIOR DESIGN

OR . . .

FILL IN THE BLANK

START A BUSINESS

KNITTING

Now that you've written down your creative calling, it's time to get started on it. One step at a time. One thing at a time.

What is one thing that will move you towards your creative calling? What is one project you'd like to start working on today?

Is it to paint and then display your work in a gallery?
To write a book?
To start your business?
To open a non-profit?
To have a consistent creative practice?
To knit beanies, for preemie babies in the hospitals?
To make jewelry or aprons or drawings and sell them on Etsy?
It's time to heartstorm...

What's the creative project you feel CALLED to most now?

. . . .

. . . .

. . . .

. . . .

. . . .

. . . .

. . . .

*If you can't decide, turn to page 234 on making decisions with clarity.

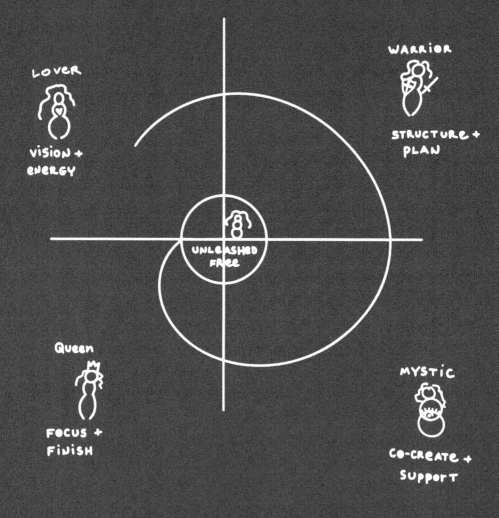

CHAPTER 2

The Unleashed
CREATIVE CYCLE

There's a natural creative energy, a cycle you move through when creating anything. You're constantly creating. Whether it's a morning practice, a relationship, a book, a workshop, a business, a painting... Whatever you're doing, you're creating using The Unleashed Cycle.

In this chapter, you'll get to know The Unleashed Creative Cycle, the steps it takes to create, and where you naturally get stuck. We all have places we normally get stuck. Let's learn where you get stuck so we can get you to finish your creative projects.

There are four parts of the Creative Cycle. We'll take a look at the four steps and the creative archetype that will help you access the energy needed for this part of the cycle. Finally, we'll take a deep dive into the steps with YOUR project.

First is ENERGY & VISION.

This first part of the cycle is influenced by the creative archetype of Lover.

In order to create anything, you need the vision to know what it is and the energy to do it. You know what it's like when you want to create something and can't get moving?

When I was a new mom, I wanted to do workshops but just the

thought of it was exhausting. I was so tired just thinking about organizing them while taking care of my kids, but I also wanted to make them a reality.

My energy wasn't up to a creation place. I was pooped out.

Your energy gets pulled in lots of different directions. It can be pulled physically, being exhausted like I was as a new mom. It can be pulled through the thoughts in your head that tell you things like: you're not good enough, or who are you to do this: these thoughts will pull you down.

Other things that pull your energy down? Confusion, overwhelm, not knowing. Frantic energy steals the energy you need to nurture your creativity and move it forward.

There are a lot of different ways we can get stuck in Energy & Vision. In this first step, we gather your energy, notice where your energy gets drained and then we build and increase it.

In this step, we use the creative archetype of Lover to get you to nurture and take care of yourself. This first step is about getting moving.

The second step is to STRUCTURE + PLAN.

This part of the cycle is influenced by the creative archetype of Warrior.

In this step, we create your structure and plan. Structure can be anything from your schedule, a strategy you put in place, or boundaries.

As creatives, we like freedom. Structure may feel boring.

Confining. But structure gives you more freedom. It allows a space for your creativity to go instead of spilling it all over. If you are painting, you have the edges of the painting. If you're writing a book, you have your book outline or idea. If you're creating a relationship there's the other person. There is a boundary. That's what structure does. It creates boundaries; it creates a container where your creative juices can play.

Schedule, strategy, planning -- all of these things are structure. They ensure you do what you want to do. Structure helps you take a look at what you're doing and then, either chunk your items down into small bites, or create a plan to get your projects done, and then also a plan for when things show up that might stop you.

If you've got lots going on in your life, structure is key. I get it. I'm a mom. I have a business. I run half marathons. I like to dance hula. I like to travel. There are all sorts of things I do. If I just let whatever happen whenever, reacting to what other people wanted, I wouldn't spend time on the things most important to me.

Structure is a way for you not only to get stuff done but also a way for you to keep what's most important to you in the forefront.

When I first started my business, I worked beyond the hours of a typical business day. I'd answer emails while my boys were doing homework, check my phone at soccer games. Now I end work when the boys wrap up school. Structure allows me to get my work done AND be present with my kids.

If you're someone that works really hard and then becomes exhausted, you need structure in place. Your pattern might be to work hard, then burn out, work hard, burn out. Or maybe you get sick a lot. Or maybe you have lots of ideas but you're not making any progress. You need structure and a plan.

Structure also means strategy. This is about doing the right things in the right order so you're not spending your time and energy on things that aren't moving you forward. It's about staying in ease for creative momentum.

In this step we use the creative archetype of Warrior to get you to create and stick with a plan, to create boundaries that will keep you focused on what's most important to you.

If you've got a million irons in the fire, you feel you're working too hard and not moving, it's time for structure. We'll create yours in Chapter 4.

 The third step is to FLOW + SUPPORT.

This part of the cycle is influenced by the creative archetype of Mystic.

This step is really about allowing. Allowing spirit, allowing inspiration, allowing flow, allowing support from others. This is the step where you're creating, things are happening -- things are birthing. You are downloading information and you are letting things flow through.

Flow can be painting, creating content for a program, or a workshop in Bali. Flow can be building your community. This part of the creative cycle is when you're actually DOING the creative part, experiencing the juiciness, and being that creative intuitive. Sacred Creativity is bigger than you. You're creating with purpose, with intention. Whether that purpose is to nurture and take care of yourself so you're a better mom or touch lives all around the world, there IS something bigger.

In this step, we tune in to your intuition and listen to what wants to be created, not just what you want to create. I can't tell you how many times I have an idea and my creation wants something different. I'll paint purple hair and my painting tells me, *No, she wants red*. I've learned to just listen. Deeper wisdom is coming through.

Part of Flow and Support is trust. Trust isn't just trusting that there is something bigger, that something will take care of you, that you're going to be given the right ideas, or that you're going to know what to say in just the right moment. Trust comes down to just one thing: YOU. Trust yourself.

Most of us have made promises to ourselves over the years. I'm going to do this or I'm going to make this happen or I'm going to make this money or I'm going to lose these pounds. Then we don't keep our promises. Over time, self-trust deteriorates. This part of the cycle rebuilds your trust.

In this step we use the creative archetype of Mystic to get you to listen to your intuition while you create and connect to the support that is around you all the time.

This is the part of the cycle for you to pay attention to...
If you're a controlling person and want to know everything that's going on. If you know you've let yourself down over and over again and you're like, enough.

If you've finally drawn your line in the sand and you are ready to start trusting and listening to yourself.

The final step is to FOCUS + FINISH.

This part of the cycle is influenced by the creative archetype of Queen.

In this step, we focus all the way to the end. This is a place a lot of people go sideways. Sideways meaning, I'm going to go another direction instead of finishing. At the end, it's common to feel bored. You want to move on to the next project already.

If you're creative, my guess is you have unfinished projects lying around your house. We all have things that are unfinished. There are things that you're going to finish through completion and then there are things you're not.

I say I got my un-finishing gene from my grandma. Grandma Sage lived to be 98. A few years ago we were going through her knitting stuff -- she's a knitter, yarn everywhere. She still has a baby sweater for Uncle Freddy (who is now 78) that doesn't have the little arms sewn on. She has the front, back, and arms, she has it all. It's done but not sewn together. Focusing and finishing.

This is especially tricky for creative women. It's like having a new boyfriend or girlfriend. At first, it's new and exciting... As opposed to the partner that's been around a while. You've hit some lulls. Worked through stuff to stay together. There are benefits to both, but not finishing projects is like hopping from one new person to another, instead of sticking with the one.

It's fine to have unfinished projects, but it's not fine to have unfinished projects that are really important to you.

How do you know what thing to focus on? There are so many amazing options. Different priorities at different times. There are times when my priority is doing a workshop. Times when my priority is finishing a painting.

Even different paintings have different priorities for me. Yeah, I've got a whole pile of paintings that aren't finished, and then I have one that I'm focused on finishing. I let myself just paint tons of stuff to be creative and free AND I have the one I am focused on.

In this final step, we use the creative archetype of Queen to get you to focus and finish the most important things for you.

Then you go back to the beginning of the cycle... building ENERGY by celebrating!!!

Most people jump straight into the next project. If you skip this step, you're missing a huge amount of available energy. You miss the momentum to carry you onto the next project.

So, when you finish something, throw yourself a party! Celebrate!

My husband Tony and I like to go out to dinner. We celebrate everything--the things that go well, as well as when we do something totally out of our comfort zone, whether we succeed or not. We celebrate finishing AND our progress.

Look at the steps of the creative cycle.
Where do you normally get hung up? Energy + Vision, Structure + Plan, Flow + Support or Focus + Finish?

PRODUCTIVE CREATIVITY

What is productive creativity? It's really two different sides of the same swing…

There's the productive side which is about action, getting things done. It's about tangible stuff. It's more a masculine energy: productive, goals, eye-of-the-tiger. This side uses the creative archetypes of Warrior and Queen.

Creativity is about spirit, inspiration, fun, out-of-the-box thinking. It's about play. It's more feminine in nature. Introspective, visionary, intuitive. This side uses the creative archetypes of Lover and Mystic.

So you've got these two different sides. Productive and creative. How do you access both sides?

Maybe you are a naturally productive person who needs creativity, or maybe you're a natural creative who needs to get productive.

You might have this idea in your head of what you want to accomplish, of what you want to do, but there's this other side that's just as important: how you want to be and feel. Many times you'll get focused on accomplishing and achieving and miss the journey. Just doing things to accomplish can feel hollow. Just being and enjoying life may not feel satisfying when you feel called to influence and make an impact.

You can be productive and get stuff done.
You can be in creative flow.
You can do both.

A couple of years ago, I just reconnected to myself to creativity. I was loving it. I was back to thinking: What do I want to be when I grow up? I knew I wanted to help women but I didn't know what that looked like. I spent the greater part of a year thinking about it, meditating about it, praying about it, waiting for an answer. I didn't know what to do. I was waiting for a sign. I was in creative flow, painting, and listening, but I wasn't moving. I was stuck.

Taking action got me moving. I didn't know what I was supposed to do, but sitting around thinking about it wasn't doing anything. I told myself, I'm just going to do one thing. Taking action started moving me. Once I was moving I could feel: this feels good, or this doesn't feel good. I was in a space of flow. I wasted time waiting. Waiting to feel safe, right, sure. Luckily, I figured it out. I took action while scared. If I hadn't, you wouldn't be reading this. That's for sure.

I see a lot of creative women wait. Waiting for stuff to happen. Waiting for it to be just right. You have to start taking action.

But then there's the other side.
The productive, doing side.

Productivity is great, except when it's not.

Years ago, I was working hard on my business. I lost me. I was in productivity, but it wasn't healthy. In fact, I ended up in the hospital with pneumonia.

I'll never forget the doctor telling me, "You are lucky to be alive right now. What are you doing here? You are too young to be in the hospital."

What was I doing there?

Laying there I realized the extent of my exhaustion and how much I'd driven myself to the point of burnout.

My husband brought my boys to visit me. My eldest came into the room and completely fell apart. He saw me in the hospital bed, an IV in my arm, the beeping of the machine delivering oxygen to me. I looked like a wreck.

I opened my arms and he climbed into my lap. I held him as he cried and I remembered. I remembered going to the hospital and visiting my mom, seeing her hooked up to the IVs and the oxygen, and remembering how scared I was.

Only she didn't make it.

So as my son was crying in my arms, I said to myself, "No. Enough. This is NOT how I'm going to live my life." I made a commitment I wouldn't let myself go to that place anymore, the place where I was focused on the doing so much I missed the living.

Maybe you're at the place I was, completely exhausted from swinging too hard to the PRODUCTIVE doing side. You're noticing your energy and recognize you need to do something different.

Maybe you're in the CREATIVE side, hearing your calling but you don't know how to start, you have too many ideas, or don't trust yourself to follow through.

Where do you naturally swing?

Do you naturally swing in the getting stuff done or do you naturally swing in the waiting for flow?

There's a sweet spot in the middle where you are listening to your intuition, tuning into your creativity, your natural flow, AND taking action. Where you're doing things on your to-do list but it's in service to what feels right. A place where you're accessing all the creative archetypes and they are in balance.

You're in the alignment space.

Let's find that spot together and see what happens.

WHEN YOU FORGET WHAT'S IMPORTANT

Let's talk.

I know how easy it is to get pulled off-center.
To get pulled into the vortex of life and forget the important things.

To get wrapped up in what's for dinner or
Finishing homework or
A work deadline or
The worries and drama of others.

To lose yourself in the DOING of life.

And yet, wake-up calls happen.
A lump on a friend's breast,
The death of your son's bird,
The anniversary of your Mom's death,
The closing of your company.

And for a moment, you wake up.
Like from a bad dream.
Crystal clear on what's important.

When you're clear, you KNOW without a doubt, you have this one great life. Time is short. You know what you want to spend your time doing.

And then you're sucked back in.
To the vortex.
You get amnesia.
I understand. I get it too.

Here's the thing sister -- Life is full of distractions. You have to create the space to return to your center over and over again, to remind yourself of what's really important.

If you don't, you'll wake up in a month or in a year or in 10 years and wonder what happened? What happened to your time?

One of the most powerful things I do to live the life I want NOW is my daily practice. I get up, meditate and pray to come back home to myself, to my center. I create DAILY. Even if I only have 5 minutes for a scribble or write in my journal. It connects me to Spirit, with Divine perspective.

This is my reminder for you.
Stop.
Listen.
Take three breaths.
It's important.
Don't go back to sleep.

Let's start creating.

First thing's first, let's find a daily practice that gives you ENERGY...

CHAPTER 3

SHE STOKES HER CREATIVE FIRE

Energy + VISION

ENERGY BASICS

In order to create anything, we need energy. But what is energy?

Think of energy as what's available to you physically, mentally, emotionally, and spiritually. It's what gives you juice, the get up and go. You've got an internal bowl full of energy. But sometimes that bowl is empty. Either you're not filling it (doing things to increase your energy) or your bowl has turned into a colander and your energy is seeping out of the holes. In this case, there are things draining your energy. We need to make sure you have an energy bowl, not an energy colander.

Let's take a look at the different types of energy and how to work with them to turn your colander into a bowl.

BODY

Body energy is how you feel physically. When I first started creating, I was exhausted. I was a mom of two young boys and rarely slept through the night. I felt tired. All. the. time. All I could do was muster up the energy to paint or write 30 minutes while the kids slept during naptime. As time went on, I started waking up in the morning early, and going for a walk before the sun rose. I started moving my body, and then things started to change. Over the next few months, I lost weight. I started eating healthier. My energy increased.

Water, sleep, food, and movement are all ingredients that affect your body energy.

MIND

Mind energy is how mentally sharp or exhausted you feel. I used to work in high-tech marketing for a start-up company in my early 20s. I remember feeling exhausted at the end of the day. I hadn't really done anything physically. Most of the day I sat at my computer, but I had spent my energy in my mind: thinking, planning, organizing. I'd grab some food, head home, and crash.

Mind energy is about thinking. Thinking out different scenarios, making decisions, weighing options, learning new things.

EMOTIONS

Emotion energy is about your feelings. Have you ever had a really good cry then felt exhausted afterward? Or worried and been unable to take action? Emotions can drain your energy, especially worry, fear, and doubt.

Thoughts about your creativity might pop in your head like, "Who am I to do this? This isn't important." These thoughts loop around in your head again and again, like a hamster on a wheel. Once you're on that loop, it moves from your MIND energy and connects into your EMOTION energy. You tell yourself all the reasons why you shouldn't be on this wheel, and bit by bit, you suck your energy away until you've convinced yourself there's no reason to even try. You feel hopeless, worried, afraid.

 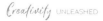

Your MIND energy is intimately connected with your EMOTION energy. What you THINK affects how you FEEL.

SPIRIT

Spirit energy is your connection to source. Spirit has its own energy. It's the energy of connection. If you're disconnected from the energy of spirit, it's like you're a battery that doesn't recharge.

Maybe you get recharged at church, in the forest, at the ocean. Maybe you get recharged when praying, meditating, or painting. How do you reconnect?

· ·

· ·

· ·

· ·

· ·

· ·

· ·

· ·

· ·

ENERGY BLOCKS

If you are stuck, scattered, or unclear, you've got an energy block.

STUCK

When I first started creating, I was tired. I was a mom with a two-year-old and a baby. I wasn't getting sleep. So for me just getting started and moving was difficult. I felt STUCK. I didn't have the energy to create.

SCATTERED

You have lots of ideas and projects. If you're working on a web-site you might be thinking about all of the pages and parts at once: you need to do the about page and write all the copy, and build the contact page. You will also probably be thinking at the same time that you need to learn how to run all the technology for a website. You are thinking about all of these things all at once. That is scattered energy. Because you've got so many ideas, you're not able to bring your energy together and then get moving.

UNCLEAR

This energy moves back and forth. It doesn't move forward. Should I do this or that? Is this the best way or that?

If you think of energy as movement,
Stuck energy moves slowwwwwwwwwww.
Scattered energy flies all over.
Unclear energy moves back and forth.

Which one of these tends to be your habit or pattern?

. . . .

. . . .

. . . .

. . . .

. . . .

. . . .

Let's get your energy moving... One of the fastest ways to move is to release what you no longer need. What's weighing you down that you could let go?

. . . .

. . . .

. . . .

. . . .

. . . .

. . . .

LOVER ENERGY

There is a part of you who knows exactly what to do when you get stuck at this part of the cycle.

A part who already knows how to
Get your energy moving,
Make a decision,
Take care of yourself,
Be patient,
Nurture and care for your energy,
Vision, and
Have self compassion.

We call this your Lover Energy.

Think of your Lover Energy as a wise part within you who knows how to best take care of you. She isn't telling you what you're doing wrong. She doesn't tell you to push more. She doesn't tell you you're running out of time. Best of all, she loves you no matter what.

Think of your Lover as your medicine when you get sick with an Energy Block.

Lover medicine is kind, encouraging, patient, and nurturing.

KINDNESS

When you're telling yourself you can't do it, you don't know how, or you've got all the reasons something isn't going to work, it's time to find the Lover within. Your inner tyrant will tell you what you're doing wrong.

Your inner Lover will tell you what you're doing right.

ENCOURAGEMENT

Think of the most encouraging mother you've ever met or seen portrayed. When their child is down, she encourages them. She'll say, "You've got this. I believe in you. Just one step at a time." This is Lover energy.

PATIENCE

You might have a made up timeline in your head on when something needs to be done. Maybe you wanted to know what to do about that character in your book two weeks ago or you know your painting isn't finished but don't know what to put in. When you start to get frustrated, it's time to invite Lover in. Let her give you guidance.
You'll know when it's time.
You're doing a great job.
There is time.
Just keep moving.

Lover isn't about rushing or needing to know. Lover trusts.

NURTURING

If you've had a time when you've driven hard, you're tired and worn and need to rest, it's time for Lover. Most times you'll tell yourself you don't have time to rest. You'll tell yourself to keep moving, create something NOW. Lover knows the best thing to do is to rest. Lover knows that space allows for the visions to come in.

When you listen to Lover you take a step forward.
Lover keeps a nourishing environment for your creative spirit. She looks out for you. Remember, Lover knows best.

LOVER MESSAGE

Now, take a moment to feel your Lover energy. Imagine putting the pen in Her hand. What does she want to tell you?

. . . .

. . . .

. . . .

. . . .

. . . .

. . . .

. . . .

. . . .

. . . .

. . . .

. . . .

. . . .

RELEASE

Sometimes you have to leave something behind to make space for the new. You need to let go in order to receive.

What change are you fighting?
What are you ready to release in order to make space for what's to come?
What is being destroyed in order to make room for creating something new?

Let it come.

RELEASE #1 : DECLUTTER

Your closet.
Your garage.
Your mind.
What is taking up space that needs to go?

Want to get your energy moving?
Make space for new ideas, relationships, and money to flow in?

I'm a fan of purging. I start with my closet. I fill bags with stuff for Goodwill. I look around and just know things need to go. And once I get rid of a few things, I'm ready to get rid of more.

Whenever you have a major change, your space wants to reflect the change, too.

When I came back from Italy, I rearranged our whole entire living room. I walked into our house after being gone three weeks and it just didn't feel right anymore. I knew it had to change because I had changed.

Our space reflects our energy.

Lou Reed, Founder of the Integrative Medicine Institute taught me the importance of not only changing our space to reflect our energy now but changing our space for who we are becoming.

I looked around my space and realized how much of my space reflected my past, things I used to love. When I really looked, it wasn't me anymore. Like the giant Japanese scroll hanging next to my bed. I lived in Japan 20 years before. It was no longer me. More important, it wasn't who I was becoming.

Changing our homes/rooms/offices to reflect who we are becoming is like creating a 3-D vision board.

Go through your house and be inspired by who you are becoming.
Get rid of clothes that don't fit exactly right.
Let go of paintings and half-finished projects that don't inspire you.
Let go of things that remind you of shoulds.
Or things holding old memories that don't feel good.

Make space for new energy to flow IN.

Here are some ideas on how to start:

Go through your things and divide everything into four piles: sale, give away, trash, and keep.
Hire your kids to run a garage sale.
Post things online.

Even if you don't have anything to replace it with, let it go.
Create a VACUUM for new things to flow in.

When I first started working with my money mentor, she had me declutter my art studio and $2,500 of unexpected income flowed in within a week.

When I started working with my sexy coach, she had me clean out a drawer in my house and, within a week, I had a major breakthrough in owning my sexual power.

One of the first things I teach in my community is to declutter things that have been sitting around for a while in order to free up energy and make room for what's available to flow in.

I've had women increase their yearly income by $10,000, sell/buy a house, get their work in galleries, or get new clients all from making space.

So here's my question for you...
What do you need to let go of in order to make room for who you are becoming? List out what physical things you are ready to release here:

. . . .

. . . .

. . . .

. . . .

. . . .

. . . .

. . . .

. . . .

. . . .

. . . .

. . . .

RELEASE #2 : FORGIVENESS

There's one thing that takes up space that you may not think about... unforgiveness.

There are people and experiences taking up space in your head, you haven't forgiven. When you hold on to them, they feed off you and drain your energy. In order to move forward, you have to let them go.

Here's how we start to free your energy...

LOVING ME LOVING YOU

LOOK AT YOURSELF

What have you done or not done that requires you to forgive yourself? How many times have you said you'd do something and haven't? How many years have you waited?

LOOK AT OTHERS

Who has wronged you in the past?
Who has told you your creativity isn't important?
Whose voice is in your head keeping you from moving forward?
It's time to let it all go.

As a meditation start coloring the heart below. Start with the center and ask yourself over and over again, *Who do I need to forgive? What do I need to let go of?*

Then, when you're ready, turn the page to your forgiveness ritual.

FORGIVENESS STARTS WITHIN

"It's one of the
GREATEST gifts
you can give
yourself,
to forgive.
Forgive
everybody."

- MAYA ANGELOU

RELEASE #3 : OLD PROJECTS

There's a reason why old projects are #3 on the RELEASE
list. These are hard to let go of, but let's give it a try anyway:

That unfinished book,
The unpainted edges on paintings,
Even the halfway done taxes.

What unfinished projects are taking up space?
What can you let go of?

. . . .

. . . .

. . . .

. . . .

. . . .

. . . .

. . . .

. . . .

. . . .

. . . .

YOUR UNFINISHED PROJECTS

. . . .

. . . .

. . . .

. . . .

. . . .

. . . .

MY ½ FINISHED PROJECTS INCLUDE...

. . . .

MY BOYS BABY ALBUMS...
THEY'RE 10 + 13 NOW

½ FINISHED PAINTINGS

. . . .

$

BOOK KEEPING REPORTS

. . . .

. . . .

ORGANIZING EMAILS

BACKYARD GARDEN

. . . .

ENERGY IN + OUT

Once you've released the old, it's time to take a look at how you're working with the energy that is coming IN and the energy that is going OUT.

What choices are you making about your energy?
What is happening unconsciously?
Where are you giving your energy away?
Who does it go towards?
What projects or tasks?

Is it saved for what you love most or spent for things that aren't your highest priorities, leaving you with little leftover?

Creativity UNLEASHED

How are you bringing energy in?
How are you nourishing yourself?
What ways are you filling your energy?

Here's the thing, you can't create if you don't have the energy
to do it. So let's take a deeper look at your energy IN and OUT.

WHAT INCREASES YOUR ENERGY?

DAILY MORNING PRACTICE

WATER

MEDITATION

GOOD FOOD

PAINTING

PRAYER

WALKS IN NATURE

WRITING

friends

DANCING

MUSIC

HUGS

READING POSITIVE BOOKS

SPACE FOR YOU TO ADD MORE HERE

Now it's your turn. Doodle, journal, or collage here...

What INCREASES your Energy?

PEOPLE. WHO?

PLACES. WHERE?

EXPERIENCES. WHAT?

Now it's your turn. Doodle, journal, or collage here...

What DECREASES your Energy?

PEOPLE. WHO?

PLACES. WHERE?

EXPERIENCES. WHAT?

CREATIVE MOMENTUM

We've released old energy, noticed where your energy is coming IN and going OUT. Now it's time to get into Creative Momentum.

Momentum is about getting moving and using the moving energy to KEEP moving.

Maybe you've had an experience where you've had a hard time STARTING. It feels like walking through thick mud. You just can't seem to get going.

Or maybe the starting is easy, but it's the KEEPING moving that's tricky.

There's a way to align your ENERGY to create momentum. Let's start now...

LOW-HANGING FRUIT

One way to get energy moving is through this practice of low-hanging fruit.

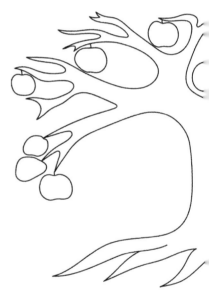

Low-hanging fruit is the easiest to pick. It is the lowest to the ground.

Here in Hawaii, we have avocado trees. They can grow to be 40 feet tall. In order to get the fruit near the top, I either need to rent a lift, get a big ladder, or get it once it's dropped to the ground. Obviously, harvesting avocados from the top of the tree is much harder than the fruit lower down. It is easiest to pick the fruit I can reach.

It's the same thing with tasks. You can get your energy moving by focusing on the things that are easy to do. Just by doing something, anything, you can get it moving. Once you start to get momentum you can come back and do the things that are a bit more difficult.

LOW HANGING FRUIT

CREATE YOUR TREE

Take a look at all your tasks, all the things you have to do for your project. Write the things that are easiest, the things that you can easily do. This is the fruit near the bottom of the tree. Write the most difficult at the top. The medium in the middle.

Next, choose one action. One low-hanging fruit to take action on first.

Go do it. Then color it in.

Do it again, and again, and again. Notice as your fruit gets colored, how your energy starts to shift with every action you take -- no matter how small or how low that fruit is.

ENERGY BOULDERS

There are times when your energy is in flow. You're going for it, super inspired. Then there are times when it feels like all your energy's been sucked out. You don't want to do anything. You'd rather binge-watch Netflix. You're in total avoidance. You know what you want to do but can't get moving.

Today we're going to look at how to move energy blocks and allow energy to flow.

When my kids were young, my second mom, Viv, came over to hang out. She could tell I was running from thing to thing. I had this frantic energy. She asked, "What are you doing?" I then shared everything I was doing, and it was a lot. She suggested we sit down and write down everything on my schedule. Once we could see everything -- all the projects and all the tasks and all the to-dos -- she invited me to think about what I wanted to do, and then decide what I wanted to get rid of if I felt like they were too much.

At the time, I was teaching three movement classes a week. I had my two-year-old and baby and I would take them with me to class. I also stayed at home with them making sure they were fed, diapers changed -- all the things. At that time I was using cloth diapers so that required washing them daily and hanging them out on the line to dry. I also tried to take showers and brush my hair. All these things at once. I felt I was drowning.

When I really looked at my schedule with Mom, I realized teaching three times a week, although it got me out of the house, wasn't serving my energy. It was draining me. I decided to teach one time a week and have someone watch the kids for me when I did that, which helped my energy increase.

You have things blocking your energy flow.

Imagine an energy river. It's clogged up. Someone built a dam across your energy river with some big boulders. One side a flow, the other a trickle.

This is your creative flow. The boulders are blocking, blocking, blocking your flow.

What are your boulders, the things blocking your creative flow?

One of mine was taxes. I had taxes that I needed to pay and accounting that was unorganized. It just hung over me, sat there, eating my energy and creating worry. What is it for you? Old paperwork, tons of emails, unsupportive relationships, old commitments, thoughts like, *I don't know what I'm doing, I'm not good enough.* Maybe worry is your boulder. Or overgiving. Overcommitment.

When looking at your boulders, it can be overwhelming. In fact, it will be overwhelming. Boulders are big and you may not know where to start. Look at one boulder you feel is going to be easiest for you to remove. Then break it down.

So for example, mine was taxes and an accountant. I started with data entry. I'd need to either find someone to hire or do it myself. I also met with an accountant and decided what I could do. Since accounting isn't my area of expertise, I'd go to someone else for help. I didn't try to figure it out myself.

Choose the boulder you're going to work with and highlight it. Once you do one task removing that boulder, draw in a stream of water coming through. Create a visual way to see you're getting energy flowing.

DAILY RITUAL

There is one thing that increases your energy more than any-thing else. It's the one thing that keeps you in momentum. What's this magic, you ask? Daily practice.

Maybe it's meditation or painting or prayer or dance or walking or swimming or singing... it's that thing that lights you up and fuels you, that connects you to spirit flow.

And yet, often it gets put behind everything else.

When that happens, it's not pretty.
You may feel frazzled or angry, bitter or depressed.
I get bitchy and feel lonely.
Sometimes I even feel sick.

It can be revolutionary to say you want me time.
It can stir things up,
Inconvenience those who lean and press upon you.
It can awaken dormant places,
Places that whisper of dreams or visions long put to rest.
And those voices you might not want to hear.
Because they also whisper of change,
What's working and many times, what's not.
And sometimes it is easier to keep walking the known path,
Even if you are discontented, it is a known discontent.

What does it take to give yourself the time?
Is it that you need to DO something to deserve it?

Because you see, there really isn't time to put it off.
There is only now.

No time for waiting.
You can only put yourself off for so long.

It's time for you...

CREATIVE RITUAL
WAYS TO INVITE IN THE DIVINE

SET AN INTENTION

PRAYER

LIGHT A CANDLE OR INCENSE

ANNOINT YOURSELF WITH HOLY WATER OR AN ESSENTIAL OIL LIKE FRANKINCENSE

MEDITATION

READ SCRIPTURE OR SPIRITUAL BOOKS OR POETRY

PICK A CARD FROM AN ORACLE DECK

ADD IN YOUR WAYS

LACEY'S STORY (ENERGY)

Meet Lacey, my sister. At one point she had six jobs. She was doing social media, she was drawing or painting pet paintings, she was working as a creative director for a bunch of kids, she was babysitting for two different families, and she wanted to start a photography business too. Whenever she tried to get moving on her photography, things would come up and she couldn't follow through. She never seemed to have enough energy or time.

Lacey is what we'd call a multi-passionate woman. She continually has an abundance of ideas. Up until we started working together, she'd try to do them ALL at once. Lacey needed some Warrior.

At first, we took a look at her schedule and prioritized what was most important. We also looked at the cost of doing all these jobs at once. She connected to Lover and cut down her jobs to make space for her photography. That allowed her to get moving.

But she soon found herself overwhelmed again. Lacey loves people and she had a hard time saying, "No." So she found herself working long hours doing favors for others. The real thing holding her energy back was not having a structure and plan to create boundaries. She found that Warrior who knew how to say No in order to get what she really wanted.

Once she got a little uncomfortable and started saying No, her photography business exploded.

It can be hard to say No. One of the excuses most people have for not doing what they want is time, waiting for things to calm down. Saying No and cutting things out will calm things down and make space for your creative spirit. And if you have a hard time saying No too, ask your Lover to remind you you're worth it and your Warrior to speak up.

MEREDITH'S STORY (ENERGY)

Meredith had written five books. Five. Have you heard of NaNoWriMo? A group of writers commits to writing their novels in one month. People make incredible progress. Meredith had done it five times and had written five novels. When we first started working together, she had five novels and didn't know which one to edit.

Each one was a book baby. Each one she had poured her time and energy into creating and crafting. She had been stuck for a long time. Which one?

We sat down together to get clear. We first looked at all five and narrowed it down to her top three, the three she loved the most. After that, we used Lover energy and I asked her which ones inspired her and gave her energy. She narrowed it down to two. Finally, in the end, when she couldn't choose, we just picked one and promised the other we'd get back to it.

Meredith ended up editing that book and could then do number two on her list, but she never would have gotten moving if she hadn't connected to what was most important to her and made a choice. She connected to the Lover within who could help her get clear on her wants and needs, who told her it was okay to make a choice.

Not making a choice eats up our energy. If you have a hard time making decisions, connect to the Lover within you.

CHAPTER 4

Structure + PLAN

WHAT IS STRUCTURE?

Structure is one of those things that creatives have a love-hate relationship with. You want freedom and yet if you don't have structure, you don't get anything done.

When I first stopped working in corporate and I stayed at home as a mom, my structure revolved around my baby. Waking up, nap time, feeding him, changing his diaper, and putting him to bed. That was my structure. As my kids grew older, I tried to figure out what to do with my time. I couldn't concentrate. I wasn't able to make things happen. I see the same thing with women who retire. They've been working a job or taking care of the family and once they retire they don't know what to do with their excess time. So nothing happens.

Structure is for you if...
You have a habit of getting overwhelmed.
You start something and then don't finish.
You have a cycle of burnout, where you work really hard and then collapse.
You try to do everything at once.

When I first started sharing my creative work, I was really excited. I was invited to paint a commissioned painting,

I had booked a solo show of all my artwork with a reception, I was giving a workshop, and I was creating my new website, all at the same time.

It was too much for me. I ended up falling apart. And, I had mediocre results. I got the commission and I had to postpone delivery because I couldn't get it done within the deadline. At the reception I was hoping for 100 people. I had 25. At the workshop I had 6 people attend and my goal was 13. And that bright and shiny new website? I threw it together. This is when I learned the bedrock of what I teach: focus, focus, focus on one thing at a time.

Being a multi-passionate woman is amazing and can sometimes be exhausting. So what do you do? You need to prioritize all the passions and all of the ideas. I know we're all multi-passionate women, we have so many ideas, things we're working on, AND pushing everything out at the same time is exhausting.

It's like kids. If you have kids, you love ALL your kids but sometimes one of your kids is more of a priority than the others because of whatever's happening with them.

A couple years ago I was working a lot of hours. I ended up burning out and getting sick. Real sick. I learned focus is important but what's also important is to create a structure with rest.

I'm going to say that again; create structure with rest.

So many times you're looking at what you're creating and what you're doing. You're in the doing of it: I'm going to get this done, I'm going to get that done. The other side of doing, though, is being, and it is just as important.

Being and Non-doing. These are the things that energize you.

When you create structure, look at BOTH sides. If you look at the swinging of the pendulum, there is a productive side where you're getting stuff done. And then, on the other side is a creative place where you're in flow. You need both. When you create your structure, have time to focus as well as rest and BE.

WARRIOR ENERGY

If you find yourself starting and stopping over and over again, if you can't get momentum or you make plans then change them because life happens, it's time to connect to your Warrior Energy.

Your Warrior Energy knows
The importance of planning,
Of creating a structure and strategy.

She's not afraid to say No.
She's the one who makes sure you are fierce when it comes to your creativity.
She defends against whatever and whoever wants to stop you, including yourself.

Think of your Warrior as the one who is standing up for your vision. She is the one who knows it is important and is willing to do whatever it takes to make it happen. She's strong, powerful, and unafraid to go against the grain.

She's the one to make sure you have a schedule to create.

She's the one to make sure you don't go to the fridge instead of sitting at your desk and writing.
She's the one who blocks off your calendar as busy.
She's the one who says No when someone wants you to volunteer for a job and it's going to eat up your creative time.
And she doesn't feel bad about it.

The Warrior uses two powerful tools:

Sword

The Warrior uses a sword of truth:
Telling the truth to yourself about what is really important.
Telling the truth to others who ask if you can shift or change your plans.
Telling the truth in the creative process, sharing what's real and authentic to you.
She doesn't put up with anything else.

Shield

The Warrior uses a shield to defend against whatever or whoever would stop you from creating:
Your kids coming into your room wanting you to make them a sandwich… Now.
Your boss asking you to work overtime.
Naysayers who tell you your work isn't important.

There is a part of you who already knows how to be a strong Warrior.

Maybe you've used that side of yourself before to defend someone or to stand up for your kids. Maybe you've used her to follow through on a commitment, or to say No when it would have been easier in your mind to say Yes.

Now it's time to access your Warrior. Imagine standing across from her. Imagine what she's wearing, what her armor looks like, how she looks at you, and how she speaks.

Draw her here...

Now, let's ask her... What do you recommend I do to tap into my Warrior Energy?

Imagine putting the pen in her hand and letting her tell you...

. . . .

. . . .

. . . .

. . . .

. . . .

. . . .

. . . .

. . . .

. . . .

. . . .

. . . .

. . . .

. . . .

SCHEDULE, RHYTHM & ROUTINE

Whether you've been inspired to write a book, crochet a beanie, or launch a business, you have to create the time to do it. That's where schedule and structure come in.

If you don't create the time, your time will be taken over with other peoples' needs and wants. Upon reflection, you may realize that you have been living this way your whole life (up until now). Planning to do something, then when someone needs you for something else, you drop your plans and say YES to someone else. It's deliciously addicting to feel needed and wanted. And we've been trained for a long time that other people are more important than our own creativity.

But you're not doing that any longer.

We have already looked at WHY you want to create. We've looked at your motivation, the thing driving you to create. Now let's create the structure so that your creativity isn't pushed to the side yet again.

Think of your schedule as a living, breathing thing. It's not going to stay still for long. There is a rhythm, a way it works with you. I have different schedules at different times of the year. My summer schedule -- when my kids are out of school -- is different from the school-year schedule. My schedule changes when I travel. And it's different when I'm on a work deadline.

STEP 1 : LET GO AND MAKE SPACE

We already spoke about letting go and making space in terms of your energy, but it's important to do this before creating a schedule as well. There are things that need to be taken off your schedule to make room for more. **What's MOST important to you? Why?**

In order to put things in proper order, you have to know what's most important to you. List out everything that's most important to you and WHY. Then order them, #1 being MOST important.

If you don't know or are having trouble, ask yourself, *If I were to die tomorrow, what would I regret not doing?*

· ·

· ·

· ·

· ·

· ·

· ·

· ·

· ·

· ·

· ·

· ·

EVERYTHING YOU'RE DOING LIST

Write down everything you're doing. Everything. From waking up to going to bed, how do you spend your time?

After you've done that, draw a line through all the things that aren't important, things that take up your time but aren't really important to you.

If you imagine you had a jar, sand, large rocks, and medium rocks, you'd have to fill that jar a certain way to fit everything in. If you filled it with sand, then tried to put in big rocks, it wouldn't all fit. Instead, you have to put the BIG rocks in first, then the medium rocks, then the sand.

PUT YOUR BIG ROCKS IN FIRST

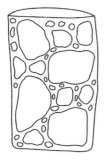

LABEL YOUR ROCKS ♡

The BIG rocks represent what's most important to you and your needs -- these are your plans and dreams and visions. If you fill your schedule with other people's needs, it's like putting sand in the jar first. You don't have space for your BIG rocks, the most important things.

Take a minute and fill out the next page.

What you highlighted as MOST important, write on your BIG rocks.

What you drew a line through would be like sand. Not important, not urgent.

Everything else are your medium-sized rocks. Not MOST important but need to be taken care of. They should fill up the remaining rocks and your time.

Look at your BIG rocks. Schedule them in your calendar. Now.

Those are the things that are most important but get put behind everything else.

Look at the sand, the things that aren't important. Delete them off your list of things-to-do list.

Look at your medium-sized rocks. These are the things that tend to take up the most time. Most of these things are important to other people, so you take care of them first.

It's time to shift this.
Either 1) delegate or 2) do these AFTER the big rocks.

I know it's easier to say than do, but I don't want you to look back with regret. Let's do this now.

STEP 2 : SCHEDULE IT

Now that you've had a chance to take some things off your plate, it's time to arrange the things you WANT to do in a way that keeps you moving.

You may have this perfect idea of you sitting in a log cabin like Henry Thoreau on Walden Pond writing your novel, but you're taking care of your aging mom and can't take off for a couple of months to write.

Schedule is about finding the right structure for YOU.
What would feel good to YOU?

Maybe 4 a.m. is a good time to create.
Or when the kids go down for a nap.
Or during your lunch break at the office.
Or before you go to bed.

Answer these questions...

What time do you want to create?

. . . .

. . . .

. . . .

When are you most energized?

. . . .

. . . .

. . . .

Is there something you're already doing that serves you, and you can easily add time to that habit to incorporate your creative practice?

. . . .

. . . .

. . . .

FLEX TIME

Look at your schedule and notice if you've scheduled any time off, time for non-doing, and just being. Studies show you're WAY more productive when you have time off. WAY. You're not a machine and can't run like one.

Eighty percent of high performers (these are people who are changing the world with their work) have a daily practice. One of my coaches takes three hours a day for himself.

If you want to make a bigger impact, you have to choose yourself.

The past couple of years, I've been doing a practice taught to me by my business coach Shanda Sumpter: Flex time. Time off. Non-doing. Play.

Three weeks working, one week off. Time to integrate, to do nothing. To allow your creative juices to flow again.

It's easy to schedule in to-dos and what other people think is important. It is something entirely different to schedule time off. Time for play and fun. Time for the creative side of you.

So as you are creating your schedule, when can you block off flex time? Weekly? Monthly? Quarterly?

Let your structure support you in taking action as well as rest.

TIGHT BUT LOOSE

How can you hold onto structure but leave space for creativity, inspiration, and play?

Tight but loose. I first heard of this from the Co-Founder of The Nia Technique, Carlos Rosas, at a training. It's about a sweet spot between freedom and form. That may mean scheduling yourself a BLOCK of time to do a list of things, but you don't have each task scheduled. That may mean scheduling time off (as well as on). Time to play, get outside. Time to let your brain loose.

Tight but loose is about creating a structure that supports you but doesn't strangle you. Here's mine at the moment...

4:30a	- 6:30a	Get up. Create. Spirit time.
6:30a	- 7:30a	Family time.
7:30a	- 8:00a	Work: team meeting.
8:00a	- 10.00a	Work: block #1
10:00a	- 12:00p	Work: block #2
12:00p	- 12:30p	Lunch
12:30p	- 2:00p	Work: block #3
2:00p	- 2:30p	Prep for next day
2:30p	- 8:00p	Family time. Workout (aka Bless my body)
8:00p		Me time. Reading. Gratitude.
8:30p		Bed.

Each block is a different project or task. I may have client sessions or coaching in our community. I may be recording trainings, writing an email, or reviewing marketing materials. Chunks allow me to tackle larger tasks and then do some of the smaller ones in the extra bits of time.

Another way I keep my schedule Tight But Loose is by assigning certain tasks to certain days. This keeps my calendar humming along. If someone wants to book an appointment with me, it will either be on a Tuesday, Wednesday, or Thursday. If I need to do writing, I'll do it on a Monday or Friday.

This makes it easier for me to make decisions as well as keeps me moving along productively. I only need to be camera-ready a couple of days a week.

Here's what my days look like:

Monday	- writing/prep for the week
Tuesday	- team meetings
Wednesday	- clients/projects
Thursday	- clients/projects
Friday	- flex (aka what needs to happen)
Saturday	- family
Sunday	- spirit

You could do something like this:

Monday, Wednesday, Friday	- write
Tuesday, Thursday	- edit

OR

Monday, Wednesday	- painting
Tuesday, Thursday	- commissions
Friday	- anything I want

Let's create your Tight But Loose Plan version 1.0.
Let's start with your theme days...

MONDAY ....

TUESDAY ....

WEDNESDAY ....

THURSDAY ....

FRIDAY ....

SATURDAY ....

SUNDAY ....

TIGHT BUT LOOSE SCHEDULE - V 1.0

TIME	MONDAY	TUESDAY	WEDNESDAY
4:00a			
5:00a			
6:00a			
7:00a			
8:00a			
9:00a			
10:00a			
11:00a			
12:00p			
1:00p			
2:00p			
3:00p			
4:00p			
5:00p			
6:00p			
7:00p			
8:00p			
9:00p			
10:00p			
11:00p			
12:00a			

THURSDAY	FRIDAY	SATURDAY	SUNDAY

TIGHT BUT LOOSE SCHEDULE - V 1.1

TIME	MONDAY	TUESDAY	WEDNESDAY
4:00a			
5:00a			
6:00a			
7:00a			
8:00a			
9:00a			
10:00a			
11:00a			
12:00p			
1:00p			
2:00p			
3:00p			
4:00p			
5:00p			
6:00p			
7:00p			
8:00p			
9:00p			
10:00p			
11:00p			
12:00a			

. . . BECAUSE LIFE CHANGES

THURSDAY	FRIDAY	SATURDAY	SUNDAY

TIGHT BUT LOOSE SCHEDULE - V 1.2

TIME	MONDAY	TUESDAY	WEDNESDAY
4:00a			
5:00a			
6:00a			
7:00a			
8:00a			
9:00a			
10:00a			
11:00a			
12:00p			
1:00p			
2:00p			
3:00p			
4:00p			
5:00p			
6:00p			
7:00p			
8:00p			
9:00p			
10:00p			
11:00p			
12:00a			

. . . BECAUSE LIFE CHANGES CONSTANTLY

THURSDAY	FRIDAY	SATURDAY	SUNDAY

STEP 3 : PLAN AHEAD FOR INTERRUPTIONS

Interruptions. They are a part of life.
Wouldn't it be nice if everything happened the way we planned?

Like if you did your art show opening, or wrote your book, or did your workshop, or put together a daily practice and everything just fell into place. Wouldn't that be nice?

It would be nice, but it wouldn't be life.
Life happens.

The thing is, you don't plan for life happening. And when it does inevitably happen, you stop.

I see it again and again. You have a beautiful dream to start a daily creative practice, and kiddos get sick and you stop. Or you decide to put your work up in a gallery, but life gets busy, and you can't put the time in so you push your timeline back for a "better time." Or you're filling a workshop, spaces don't fill, and you pull back instead of pushing through, sure it's a sign from the universe.

Here's the deal. Life happens. When blocks are thrown in our creative path, it isn't a sign to stop. It's a sign to keep moving forward. It's a sign you're on the creative path because let's face it, it takes some pushing to birth anything.

You just need to figure out how to walk your creative path in the midst of life.

I know what it's like for life to take you out.
I felt that way when my mom passed,
when I miscarried,

when my babies were young and I wasn't getting rest, when I was so busy with my work, I forgot myself.

When life feels like too much, you need a plan. And so that's what we're gonna do.

Sometimes when you're answering your creative calling you've got to build in a structure that doesn't allow other people to get in. Think of it like you've got the most amazing creative treasure and it's up to you to make sure no one steals it.

So you build a castle and a moat and get some warriors to protect it. You make sure you've got plans in case of attack.

Same thing with your creativity.

CREATING SPACE + BOUNDARIES
PROTECT YOUR CREATIVITY

DRAW BRIDGE

MOAT OF PROTECTION

If you don't put up some boundaries, you'll let OTHER PEOPLE decide whether your work is important, whether it will amount to anything, whether you can make it or not. If you allow the wrong people to have a say, they'll say the same stuff that critic in your head is saying and next thing you know, you've decided NOT to answer your creative calling anymore.

You're allowing others to influence your mind in the wrong direction.

If you don't put up boundaries, you'll be interrupted over and over again by what other people need from you. You'll be creating and next thing you know, you're getting a phone call and an hour later, you still haven't created, and it's time to go do something else.

So here are three ways to set up boundaries to keep your creative calling protected and loved.

1.   DO NOT DISTURB

Make sure your peeps know when you're creating, it's SACRED TIME. My kids and husband know when I'm going to my studio, and they also know I'm not to be disturbed unless it's an emergency. I've explained when it is okay to be disturbed and when it is not. This means if the kids can't find the milk or their fishing pole line, they're gonna have to wait. This means if someone is bleeding or something is on fire, I can be interrupted.

In order to remind them, I make a

DO NOT DISTURB - I AM CREATING sign.

You can make yours here, rip it out, and hang it on your door. Voila!

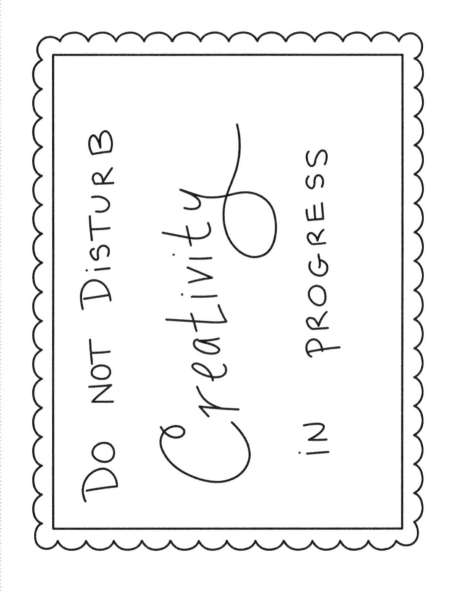

2. CREATE THE PERFECT YUMMY CREATIVE ENVIRONMENT

What can you do to plan ahead? I like to....

Have my stuff ready.
This means I have a canvas, water, paints, and brushes set up. All I have to do is pick up the brush and GO. No need to DO anything to start creating.

Put my phone away.
No notifications, calls, texts. I think of what it used to be like 20 years ago when we all weren't at the beck and call of everyone. If someone wanted to reach us, we had to be by the phone. I figure, if it's important, I'll get to it in an hour.

You can put your phone in a box, put it in airplane mode, turn off notifications. SO many options to not be disturbed.

Here is my phone box.

MY PHONE BOX

Side (Shiny Object) Project:
Make your own phone box.

Let people know you're entering the creative realm.

That means you'll be unavailable (see #1 above).

Make yourself a cup of tea.
I put together refreshments so I don't use the excuse I need some beverage or food to stop creating. Mostly I make myself a cup of hot tea and have a dark chocolate bar handy.

MY YUMMY CREATIVE ENVIRONMENT INCLUDES....

PAINTING STATION SET . UP

NATURAL LIGHT

CUP OF EARL GREY TEA

CANDLE

GOOD MUSIC

JOURNAL

CHOCOLATE

GLITTER

Your YUMMY CREATIVE ENVIRONMENT includes ...

3. GET GOOD AT SAYING NO TO GOOD SO YOU CAN SAY YES TO GREAT

CReaTeS

FReeDOM

People ask you to do stuff all the time. It's time to get good at saying NO.

Sure, we've created some space and cleared some clutter from your schedule, but unless you start saying NO, your schedule is gonna fill up again with things you don't want in there... like volunteering to pull weeds in your kid's school garden.

Here's a list of things I say no to on a regular basis to make room for my creativity:

Laundry
Dishes
Volunteer projects at school
Someone wanting to "pick" my brain
Facebook
Instagram
Pinterest
Binge-watching a new Netflix series
Pulling weeds
Email
Requests to donate my time
Putting together extravagant dinners
Ironing
Bookkeeping

Requests to write articles for others
Collaborations (unless it's WAY juicy)
Here are things I still find the time for AND do my creativity:

Working out
Eating well
Calling my family
Reading books
Sexy time with hubby
Dates with my kids

GOOD, BETTER, BEST

One of the main things that will take you out of creating is your THINKING.

Setting expectations that are WAY too big, then beating your-self up afterward when you don't meet them is a sure-fire way to take yourself out of your creativity. It's an expectation hangover. Here's an example: you tell yourself you're gonna write a book in a month, then you only get chapter one done and you say, *Why bother?* So you stop.

We're gonna set up a new way of thinking to make sure that doesn't happen.
It's called good, better, best.

I put together good, better, best for everything I do. It keeps me from getting derailed if I don't do as much as I want.

When I'm enrolling into my yearlong mentorship program, my good goal is one I know I can meet. Better is a little stretchy.

Best would be tough to meet, but it's possible. It's the same when I'm enrolling for a workshop.

And here are some other examples:
How much I'm writing in a week.
How many days per week I'm working out.
How much time I'm painting.
How many pieces I'm finishing.
How many galleries I'm reaching out to.

Everything on your list can be broken down into good, better, best.

Progress NOT Perfection

Now it's YOUR turn.

. . . .

. . . .

. . . .

When you think of your creative calling project, what do you
want to get done? What would be good enough (good)?

. . . .

. . . .

. . . .

What would be better than that (better)?

. . . .

. . . .

. . . .

What would be amazingggg (best)!!!?

. . . .

. . . .

. . . .

It's good to know you're good enough.
To find satisfaction in the doing, even if it's just a little.

Five minutes, day after day, adds up.
It can be one call,
One paragraph,
One painting session,
One email,
One conversation.

Just do it.
And let it be good enough.

It doesn't help you to beat yourself up
Over what you haven't done up to this point
Or what you should have done
Or all the things you have yet to do.

Just keep moving sister.
Just keep choosing you,
And what you love,
And what you dream.

PERMISSION SLIPS USE AS NEEDED

PERMISSION TO DO ONLY WHAT'S MOST IMPORTANT

PERMISSION TO NOT GET IT RIGHT

PERMISSION FOR IT TO NOT BE PERFECT

STRATEGY - WORK SMARTER, NOT HARDER

There is a myth that says you need to work HARD.
That success comes with PUSHING.
That you should be doing MORE.

I used to think if I wasn't working HARD, I needed to do more.
I would make myself busy because I thought by being busy, I'd
get more work, sell more paintings, bring more people to my
workshops, finish more. I thought being successful equaled
busyness.

But it didn't. Instead, it scattered my energy, I didn't make good
money, AND I landed in the hospital.

It is easy to get into the habit of working HARD and thinking
you need to be doing a lot. Instead, work SMART.

Here's what working SMART looks like:

SMART = Having a creative practice at the same time every day.
HARD = Changing it every day so it doesn't become a habit.

SMART = Hiring help for things you're not good at so you can
do your art.
HARD = Trying to do it ALL yourself.

SMART = Having a plan for working with people AFTER you
lead a workshop.
HARD = Teaching workshop after workshop with no recurring
income.

When you look at your creative project, are you making it harder
than it needs to be? If so, what can you do instead?

Here's some space for your SMART, not HARD ideas:

. . . .

. . . .

. . . .

. . . .

. . . .

. . . .

. . . .

Busy is a great distraction.

The thing about busyness and hard work - it's glorified, socially acceptable. We all do it. It's our greeting. How are you doing? Busy. You? Busy. When we slow down, take breaks or time off, it has to be earned first.

Busyness is a distraction. You might get praised for it but you also might lose your friends, partner, or kids. You might get really sick. When that happens, it's a wake-up call. It can slow you down enough for you to realize that busyness is not the way.

Busyness is surface level. Next. Next. Next. No intimacy. No opportunity for self-reflection.

Busyness is never-ending. Our lives are built upon rhythm. The heavens are on rhythm. Mother earth has her seasons. Waxing and waning of the moon. As women, we have natural cycles.

Busyness takes your rhythmic body and puts it on perpetual summer. Forever sunny. Go. Go. Go. And do you know what happens when you're busy all the time?

You feel rushed, stretched, frazzled. And you start to get snappy.

Consider it a warning sign... a bright flashing red light. Look at what you are asking yourself to do. Your inner snappy side has your best interest at heart... and she'll let you know when you're not listening and need to slow down.

UNLEASHED TIP

List out your warning signs here so you know how to recognize them.

. . . .

. . . .

. . . .

. . . .

. . . .

. . . .

TRACKING & MOTIVATION

There's this funny thing that happens when you start your creative projects. You're excited, inspired, riding a high, then life sets in, and you find a million other things to do instead. You have to set up a system to make sure you KEEP doing your creative work. Welcome to tracking. There are two ways to motivate yourself: rewards and peer pressure.

REWARDS

I recently rediscovered REWARDS with my kids. I'd been trying to come up with some system to motivate my kids. Hello, rewards chart.

We made a chart of everything I wanted them to focus on. DOING things like homework, reading, making their beds. BEING things like kind and generous. Also qualities I wanted them to focus more on... for my youngest that's making decisions quickly and asking for what he wants. For my oldest that was helping his younger brother.

We then came up with rewards. Things that would KEEP them moving. My oldest LOVES fishing so his rewards included fishing lures, fishing day trips, and a 24-hour camping fishing experience. The more stickers he earned, the closer he got to his reward.

The kids were on fire. Reading two hours a day to get extra stickers. Their grades were up. They were happy, connecting, and getting rewarded for what they wanted to be doing.

I thought maybe it could work for me.
I started easy. With drinking more water. And writing.
I rewarded myself with manicures, massages, a retreat date, guilt-free reading time. I loved it.

And with this success, I decided my clients needed it too. And you may have guessed, tracking towards rewards worked for my clients too. My clients wrote books, painted, lost weight, and built their creative businesses, one sticker, one heart, and one smiley face at a time.

REWARDS CHART
WHAT PRACTICE DO YOU WANT TO REINFORCE?

TO DO ↓	M	T	W	TH	F	SA	SUN

GOOD = ♡   BETTER = ♡♡   BEST = ♡♡♡

5 ♡ =   100 ♡ =

20 ♡ =

PEER PRESSURE

The other way to motivate yourself is by PEER PRESSURE. It's less popular but still has its purpose.

It's okay if you need some. I do.
I don't like to look bad. So I'll declare something to people I really admire. For instance, I will tell my creative sister I'm going to finish my painting next week and post it. Then there is NO WAY to back out. I'll do whatever I have to do.

Another way I've created some helpful peer pressure for myself is by creating something I need in my own life. For instance, when I was changing my creative practice, I put together an online course teaching how to create your daily practice. I'd meet women online daily and created. It gave me accountability, and at that moment it was just what I needed.

Another thing I've done is tell a friend I'll pay them $$$ if I don't do what I say I'm going to do. Like, I'll pay you $50 if I don't write three times this week. If you like not wasting money, this one might motivate you as well.
Let's heartstorm.

What are some ways you can motivate yourself that may be

a bit uncomfortable...
KAREN'S STORY (PLAN)

Choose 1 and
declare it to
someone now.

Karen lives in Italy. She's a mom of a little boy, and she came to me when she wanted to work on her art. She had started her work as a professional artist and within a short amount of time, her mom and sister passed away. She shut down. All the momentum she had created stopped.

For a couple of years, she just couldn't do her work and then her dad passed as well in an accident. She said to me, "Amber, I don't want to put my stuff on hold anymore. I know I need to do it."

She asked herself, "Why do I keep putting my art on the back burner?" She wanted to keep her art moving, in the midst of everything that was happening. We started working together and the first thing we did was access the creative archetype of Lover and used art to work with her grief. So instead of thinking about creating artwork professionally later, we decided to do it now. Be in the grief of just losing her dad and let whatever art was coming, come. Letting art be a support.

Later, she had to go to California to sort through his whole house and his belongings and put the house on the market to sell. We started working with the Warrior because her schedule was changing again, and her structure had to change as well. She was going somewhere else, something totally different was happening. So we looked at small things, micro ways her warrior could stand up so her work and practice didn't get put aside.

Later her son was home from school for the summer, so then she wanted to learn how to create AND spend time with her son.

Just like Karen, your structure and schedule are always changing. Things are coming, things are going. What can you do to create structure so when life is happening you keep moving on what's most important for you?

Shortly afterward, Karen sent two collages to a gallery in Berlin. Some of those collages were her work with her grief. If she had completely stopped when her grief took hold, she wouldn't have been ready when that opportunity came to her. Instead, she let her art help her through her grief, and in turn her grief helped her.

What structure do you need, so your creative project doesn't get put at the bottom of the pile?

LARA'S STORY (PLAN)

Lara is magical. She brings fun, play, and childlike wonder to her workshops. When we first met, she had workshops and retreats planned, one after another. She'd do a painting and play workshop then right after she finished, she'd start reaching out to fill the next one. She was constantly sharing her events and never seemed to get traction.

We connected to the Warrior and created a strategy to build and fill, so one event would flow into the next. She filled her weekend workshops then invited those at the workshop to her weeklong dolphin retreat.

Recently, she used Warrior again to create a plan and fill her nine-month Passion Portal Program by inviting women from her events and offerings to play together.

What ways can you make things easier for yourself? Strategy looks at how to weave things and your energy together instead of having things flow separately.

WHAT IS INTUITION?

Flow + SUPPORT

Intuition.
Sixth sense.

Most of my life I didn't think I had that power.
Maybe, like me, you were raised to second guess your intuition.
Maybe you think, "If it doesn't make sense, it's not real."
Maybe you want to believe that intuition is possible in general, but you think it's not for you, you never received that intuitive thing others have.
Or maybe you know how to listen to your intuition, but you just don't act on it.

The power of intuition is available to EVERYONE. You just need to learn how to use it. And it takes a different kind of listening than what you're used to...

When you're aligned with your intuition, things become easier. You meet the right people, at the right time. You're in the flow. You're not working on your own. You're able to see more possibilities.

Here's the secret. Intuition is really about listening to Spirit.
It's about CO-CREATION.
Spirit is here to help and you need to listen.

OR you can do it the other way.

I did that for years. Graduated from college. Great job. Working my way up the corporate ladder, working 60- to 70-hour weeks, not listening. When I had a week off work, I could hear it, but doing what my intuition was telling me to do felt too over- whelming. I thought if I listened, my whole world might turn upside down.

Instead, years later I wondered how I got to where I was. I had lost my adventurous self. I was serious and only focused on production and success. And it felt hollow. And lonely.

Then I started listening again.

It led me to creativity and women's work.
It slowed me down.
It showed me how I could make a difference, but not just from my own effort.

And now, I use it all the time. I listen...
Before I write to you.
When I think of the women I want to work with.
When I hire my team.
When I bring on collaborative partners.
When I paint.
When I talk to my kids.
When I pick up the phone to call someone.
I listen.

So HOW do you tap into the power of intuition? It starts with listening, but there's more.
STEP 1 : **LISTEN** TO YOUR INTUITION

We all hear our intuition differently. Most times that listening doesn't happen with your ears. Maybe your intuition speaks to you through all of your senses: what you see, hear, touch, taste, or smell. Maybe you can feel it in different parts of your body. Maybe, you just have a knowing.

It's like a radio station. You pick it up on your own wavelength. What is YOUR way to hear your intuition?

Write here...
If you're having trouble figuring this out, think of a time you knew something was going to happen or you felt something bad was coming. How did you know?

YOUR INTUITION STATION
HOW DO YOU HEAR IT?

VISION

HEARING SOUNDS

NATURE

SMELLING

INTUITION RADIO

YOU JUST KNOW

TASTE

STOP
SEE SIGNS

FEEL IN BODY · SENSES

OTHER (YOUR WAY)...

STEP 2 : **LEARN** TO **TRUST** IT

How do you tell the difference between your normal thoughts and intuition? Just like any relationship, you have to build trust.

. . . .

. . . .

. . . .

. . . .

. . . .

. . . .

You have to get to know it and know what it sounds like.

In order to build trust, I recommend you practice paying attention to your intuition. When you listen to your intuition, what happens? When you don't listen and do something else, what happens?

Start tracking your intuitive nudges.

You want to build up confidence in your intuition, even when it makes no sense.

7 REASONS TO TRUST MY INTUITION...

1 – It connects me to Spirit which knows A LOT more than me.

2 – It accesses information from my subconscious which gets 11 million bits of information per second instead of the 200 bits my conscious mind takes in.

3 – It has my best interest at heart.

4 – I don't have to do it all myself and that feels good.

5 – It makes decision-making WAY easier.

6 – It warns me of dangerous situations and people.

7 – Add your reason in here:

STEP 3 : **ACT** ON IT

This is the hardest step for most of us. Taking action when it doesn't make sense or when your lived experience has told you it's not going to work out. It takes

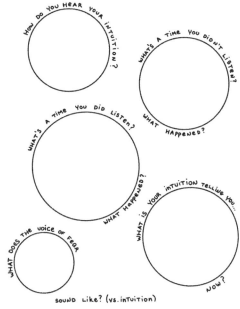

bravery to listen to a part of you who hasn't been honored in centuries.

Start to practice using it for small things... the clothes you decide to put on for the day, the paint colors you choose, the person you decide to call. Feel how your intuition resonates in your body. What's the outcome: what happens when you DO take action. When you practice acting on your intuition for small things you will have more confidence for acting on it for ALL things. Then, when you feel the nudge and it's something big like investing in your art or starting a business, you'll have practice and will be able to trust it.

Here's how I consciously tune inwards to LISTEN, TRUST, and ACT on my Intuition:
I close my eyes,
Put my hand on my heart,
Ask my intuitive self for 1 small baby step,
And then, I do what I'm told.
(No matter what)

I've ignored my intuition too many times before and I KNOW how that feels. So here's to tapping into the power of intuition for more ease and joy.

What does your intuition want you to do? Listen, trust, act. You've got this.

MYSTIC ENERGY

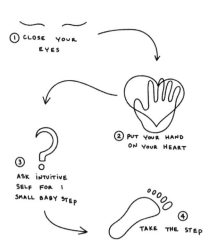

LISTEN , TRUST , ACT ON INTUITION
HOW TO TUNE INWARDS + DO IT

① CLOSE YOUR EYES

② PUT YOUR HAND ON YOUR HEART

③ ASK INTUITIVE SELF FOR 1 SMALL BABY STEP

④ TAKE THE STEP

If you have trouble tapping into flow,

Connecting to your intuition,
Knowing what Spirit is calling
you to do,
Calling on support,
It's time to activate your
Mystic energy.

she looks for spirit signs

The Mystic is the one who trusts
the unseen realms.
She knows in her bones she is always
connected to Spirit, that her creative
work is really about allowing Spirit to
channel through her. She trusts timing,
Spirit, and herself when the unknown
appears because she is a master of trusting.

She knows she cannot do it alone, that she was made to be
in connection.

The Mystic listens to her intuition, trusts her calling and acts on
it. She calls on her support and connects to Spirit to tap into
flow. She uses ritual and allows space and time for integration.

There is a piece of you who already knows.
This is the Mystic.
Typically if you get stuck on this part of the creative cycle, you're
too much in your head. You're trying to figure things out. This
stops flow. This limits what the Divine is able to create through
you.

The Mystic asks you to let go of figuring things out, to let go of
control and to allow the flow. The Mystic asks you to just BE.

Let's connect with her.
Place one hand on your heart and one hand on your lower belly.
Close your eyes and take a few deep breaths.
Breathe in trust. Breathe out anything else.

Breathe in love. Breathe out anything else.
Breathe in support. Breathe out anything else.

Slow yourself down to listen.

Imagine connecting to your Mystic within, the one who is wise,
who trusts Spirit and flow, who doesn't worry.

Imagine sitting across
from her breathing
together. What does
she have to say about
how to access your
Mystic energy within?

SUPPORT

—

WHO'S
IN YOUR

SHE LISTENS TO BUBBLES OF SPIRIT

CANOE?

Have you ever paddled a canoe with someone? If you're not paddling together, it's a mess. You're either smacking each other's paddles or your turning in circles.

Think of your creative project like your canoe. You're the person steering your project. You need to make sure you've got people paddling WITH you.

You've already got people in your canoe. They may be paddling with you. They may be paddling against you. They may just be sitting there, dead weight in your boat.

When you're creating ANYTHING, you need a solid crew.
People who will support your vision.
People who will encourage you when you want to give up.
People who believe it's possible.
People who will challenge you to be better, to do better.

Here's who you DON'T want on your crew:
Your Dad who thinks this creative work won't pay the bills.
Your friend who wants to tell you "realistically" what she thinks.
Your roommate who invites you to go drinking late at night when she knows you've got a workshop the next morning.

You want to be around others who lift you up, who inspire you, who get you to think differently.

When there is a group of powerful creatives, holy moly. Shit is gonna happen.

Time to take a look at who is currently on your paddling crew and who you need to replace...
ASKING

Draw the support currently in your canoe. These are the people you are listening to. They may be supportive and they may not.

CURRENT   SUPPORT   CREW
WHO IS IN YOUR CANOE?

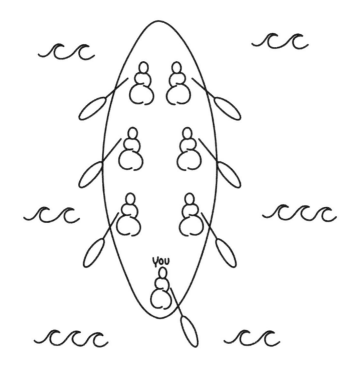

Now who would you like in your canoe? These may be people already in your life you want to listen to and connect with more, or they may be positions yet to fill.

WHO DO YOU WANT TO BE?

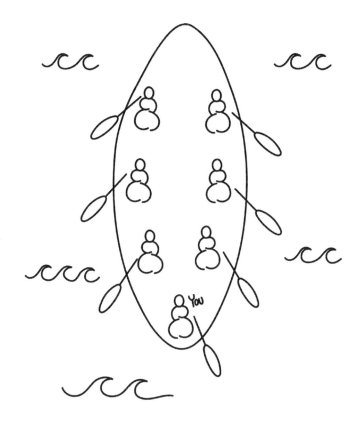

How much support can you receive? How much can you ask of others?

When you ask people to give, new possibilities unfold. When you ask, there is less burden and more ease. When you ask, it's no longer about independence, it's about interdependence and connection. You just have to open up your
mouth to ask.

And yes, I know that's the hardest
part. Magic begins with the asking.

Asking got my first painting in a
gallery,
A scholarship to work with my mentor,
The best accountability partner,
My bookkeeper.
Asking kept me injury-free when
working out.
Asking my clients what they love has
kept me working with them for years.

I used to think asking made me weak. I should be able to soldier on myself, not need anyone. But that's not the way to freedom. The way to freedom is by receiving the abundance and love and support and ideas all around you. CO-CREATION. So what are you going to ask for?

Where do you need help? What do you want? Who has already got what you want? Who already knows what you need to know? Who can take things off your plate? Whose ideas and experience could you use?

It's time to ask.

Have you felt scared by your creative

WHAT ARE YOU GOING TO ASK FOR (OR , WHAT DO YOU NEED HELP WITH)?	FROM WHOM?

calling? Maybe you've had
thoughts like these:

This is too much. I can't do it.
Maybe I should go back to the life
I was living before.

But calling gnaws at you. And pushing
it down doesn't help. Not really.
I get it. I just want to remind you
that these questions are part of
the creative process.
That moment when it feels TOO big.
That moment of second guessing.
When that moment comes, remember...
You're on your creative path.

You're just about to
give creative birth.
Keep breathing sister.

CREATIVE RITUAL

Creative ritual is about taking your creative practice and inviting in the divine. It's about recognizing that creativity is more than just something to do. It is your connection to Spirit.

Ritual is about the sacred.
It's about consistency.
It's about opening a doorway.

When you're creating, how can you intentionally co-create?

How can you add ritual into your creativity?

INTEGRATION

It can be easy to just power through things to learn, learn, learn, do, do, do. There is a difference between learning and living. Bringing our learnings into our lives. Moving from thinking about something to becoming it.

I remember a couple of years ago feeling confused about my spiritual path. The one I grew up with wasn't working anymore and it felt like my foundation was cracking from underneath me. I was so HUNGRY to connect to my spirit. I read book after book about spirituality. I'd power through them in a day or two and move on to the next. Searching. Searching.

Eventually, I felt FULL. Like if I read any more, my head would explode. Like I had filled up enough and now was a time to bring it out of my head and into my life. To integrate.

In the middle of a visualization I was leading for my mentorship group, this is what I got:

A NEST.

Then it hit me.

You need to create an environment for yourself like a mother does for her chicks... where you're well-nourished, body, mind, and spirit. You need it set up so the things that feed your soul are easy to do, no effort needed to make it happen. Shifting the energy to abundance and flow, setting up an environment of trust and receiving. Of INTEGRATION.

Here are four ways to Build Your Nest...
(aka. Integrate what you learn into your life):

1. MAKE IT **EASY**

If you know what you want to change, make it easy. Think of

all the things that have kept you from doing it in the past and create a plan so you don't fail before you start.

If you know you want more creativity in your life but... You're too busy, you get caught up, you forget, you feel guilty... you need to find a way through what stops you into what you want.

Here is what I do: Set my journal, markers, and mini watercolor set in a basket next to my bed so when I wake up, they are there within reach.

Think about how to easy-ify things for yourself. Want to paint? Have your canvas, water, paints, and brushes ready so you can walk in and paint even if you only have ten minutes. If you want to start drinking more water, set a glass near your bed so you wake up and take a swig. If you want to start walking in the morning, set your alarm earlier and put it halfway across the room with your clothes and shoes next to it so you have to get up.

Do you see what I'm talking about? Look at what is going to stop you before you get started and have a plan to make it easier.

2.   MAKE IT FEEL **GOOD**

I avoid change if it's gonna feel icky.
How do you shift it? Make it fun.
How can you make the change you want even more appetizing, more yummy? Think cherry on the top.

3.   MAKE **ROOM**

If you have everything planned back to back, there isn't room for integration. Part of integration is letting your brain have some downtime to rewire on the inside. This is where flow comes.

This is why people are more productive and effective when they take vacations and breaks. This is why I take the last week of the month off. As my husband says, slow down to speed up.

This is about letting the energy of control go, trusting, and making room to receive. You can't receive if you are doing it all yourself. So let go. It feels sooooooo good.

4.   MAKE IT **SACRED**

My transformation hasn't come by me MAKING things happen. It has come through surrendering to Spirit (God, Source, Divine). By tapping into the power of something bigger than myself, shift happens.

Some of my biggest transformations have been during ritual, ceremony, and prayer. Letting the Mystery take the lead.

What can you do to integrate this teaching, this book, and not just let it be another bit of information sitting in your head? Write your ideas here:

MARIA'S STORY (SUPPORT)

When she was very young, Maria got a story from her mother that she wasn't creative. When she was five, she showed her mom one of her works and her mom said, "That's ugly." From that point on, she told herself, I'm not creative. I'm not gonna paint.

I did an in-person workshop and she called me beforehand. She wanted to do it but she was totally petrified. I told her, "Honey I've got you, I'm gonna help you through this." She came to the workshop and connected to Mystic opening to support.

When she picked up the paintbrush for the first time, I could feel her anxiety. She was so nervous. Every day she leaned into the support. Once those three days passed, she felt free.

This is what happens when we face our fear AND move through it, when we take even one step into that space. Immense amounts of energy come. There is freedom. A lightening. Fear collapses us. It makes us smaller. By moving with it, by taking a step, space opens up.

"Before I worked with Amber, I was frightened about even touching a brush, not even mentioning painting. Just the thought would make me tear up. I thought I was just bad at doing any art. Our time together has broken those walls. I'm painting and loving it. It allowed me to trust myself. Now I'm not afraid."

Maria's now an unstoppable creative force. Her paintings have been featured at music festivals and shows, all through leaning in to support and trusting her creative flow.

CARM'S STORY (SUPPORT)

Carm had been a nurse her whole life, but there was this other side of her that wanted to create. When we started working together, we looked at that story. She said, "I feel like I'm dying. I've got to get my creativity out."

Part of what was keeping her in her nursing career was this story about her mom. Her mom was a nurse and had passed young. Carm felt disloyal leaving nursing. By staying, there was a connection with her mom.

We looked at creating a new story. We connected to the Mystic and looked at the parts of her mom that would con-nect to her new story of her creative self. We found her mom was super courageous and did things outside the box. She didn't care what people thought. We tapped into that side of her mom, the one with the creative side, the one that wouldn't care what others thought, and integrated that into her creativity. Carm held onto her Mom's courageousness and beauty. She felt her Mom's support. She left her nursing career and started creating.

Since Carm wrote this, she's co-creating with her creative spirit. It's a way of life. She is painting, sewing, and published a book focusing on spiritual art.

"I feel more direction and focus as I'm moving in the direction of my dreams. I feel that I've let go of the fake me and the real authentic me is emerging, I feel totally supported. I feel hope and joy."

SHINY OBJECT

CHAPTER 6

SHE FOCUSES ON HER QUEEND

FOCUS + FINISH

SYNDROME

Have a bunch of unfinished projects?
Loads of ideas but you can't get moving?

I know how it goes.
You have an idea.
You're excited. This is the next BIG thing.
Then once you're in it, it starts to get boring,
Hard, uncomfortable,
And all of a sudden, you have another great idea.
You stop everything you were doing and focus on your next
BIG thing.

Shiny Object Syndrome strikes again.
This looks like a bunch of unfinished paintings,
Or unfinished books, poems, knitted sweaters,
A business idea that you started... then decided to do some-
thing different.
You go from one idea to the next, the next, the next.
And don't finish or ever get momentum and that feels crummy.

I get it.
That was me for most of my life.

When I first started my business, Shiny Object Syndrome almost put me out of business.

At first, I led small women's circles, six women around my dining room table.
Only, I wanted to impact more women, so I stopped circles and started three-day workshops.
Only I wasn't making money, so I stopped workshops and started selling a one-on-one program.
Only I sucked at selling, so I stopped the one-on-one program and started a six-month, lower-priced group program.
Only, I wanted to work with women longer, so I stopped the six-month program and started a year-long program.
Only I didn't feel like women were getting as much as they could, so I...
It was at this point I recognized my pattern.

Anytime things would get hard or uncomfortable or boring, I'd move on.
I'd quit.

No wonder I wasn't building momentum.
And because I'm a creative multi-passionate woman, I had no problem coming up with plenty of ideas of what I should do instead.

I see this all the time.
Creatives and healers who have a business and change it over and over again,
Artists who start a painting series, then halfway through begin another,
Workshop leaders who teach a workshop, then do a different one and another.
Writers who change their book idea halfway through.

When I recognized my pattern, I decided to make my year-long program the best it could be. I stopped dabbling and taught the same program year after year. More and more people got better and better results. Word spread. We sold out. That would have never happened if whenever I got bored or uncomfortable, I'd changed the program. I would have missed mastery.

What if you moved from dabbling to mastery?
Instead of dating new idea after new idea, you married your idea?
Committed.

You finished the paintings.
Taught the same workshop again. Better.
Finished the book.
Continued selling your program or offering until YOU got better.
What could change?

What if I choose the wrong thing?
What if the other idea is better?

What if you go all in?
What could happen?

UNLEASHED TIP

What to do with all your Shiny Object Ideas.
It's not like when you decide to focus on one thing that everything else goes away, right?

I created a journal page called Amber's Shiny Object List.
Every idea goes in there.
It's an energetic space holder for what wants to come.

Mine currently holds over 111 ideas including...

- A fantasy series about a woman and her connection to a race of dragons
- A painting series of powerful iconic women to inspire young girls
- A journal for terminal parents to leave their children for guidance and wisdom
- A Woman Unleashed Planner/Journal
- Woman Unleashed Online Retreats in multiple languages

You've probably got ideas for 10 lifetimes.

Let's do what you can with this lifetime.

YOUR SHINY OBJECT LIST

1. . . . .

2. . . . .

3. . . . .

4. . . . .

5. . . . .

6. . . . .

7. . . . .

8. . . . .

9. . . . .

10. . . . .

11. . . . .

12. . . . .

13. . . . .

14. . . . .

What if you actually finished?
What would change?
How would you feel?

....

....

....

....

....

....

....

....

....

....

....

....

QUEEN ENERGY

There is a piece of you who knows how important it is to focus
and follow through, who can see the big picture,
Who doesn't get distracted by the latest new thing to come
along,
One who has long-term perspective.

Welcome to Queen Energy.

Your Queen stands for what she desires until that desire is ful-
filled. She rules her Queendom (Creative world) with love AND
commitment. She doesn't change her mind day to day depend-
ing on what she feels at that moment. She knows feelings come
and go and she takes action based on her commitments.

Being a Queen isn't always fun. A princess can change her
mind and the decisions don't solely rest on her shoulders, but
a Queen carries all the responsibility and power.

You have a Queen within you.
She is standing for your completed project.
She listens to her advisors the Lover, Warrior, and Mystic but
ultimately, she decides.
When stuff comes up that is uncomfortable, she doesn't hide.
She makes the tough decision. There is no one coming to
save her.

She's not a tyrant queen demanding things be done or else.
She's not a princess waiting for someone else to help her.
She rules her Queendom with grace and ease.

If you struggle finishing what you start either because you keep
jumping from idea to idea OR if you don't finish because you
keep working on your project long after it's done (because it's
just not right yet), it's time to activate your Queen.

Imagine the side of yourself who is a gracious ruling leader, the one who believes in you and never gives up or abdicates her throne to make others happy or make herself more comfortable. Imagine your wise ruler within.

She has something to tell you about how you create, things to know about this creative project. Let's sit down together and hear what she has to say...

. . . .

. . . .

. . . .

. . . .

. . . .

. . . .

. . . .

. . . .

. . . .

QUITTING - THE ONLY WAY TO FAIL IS TO STOP

Sometimes taking action towards your dreams feels like you're in the flow. It feels easy. It feels peaceful. Other times it feels like you are walking through thick mud. It feels hard. It feels stressful.

How it feels doesn't determine whether or not you should do something.

You know what these feelings telling you to stop are really saying? You're doing the work.

Imagine if those times you stopped, you didn't.
Imagine what you would have accomplished.
How you would have felt.
How many lives you would have changed.

During those times when you felt called towards something big,
Imagine if you just kept moving forward, little by little.

You can only fail at something if you give up.

THE ONLY WAY
TO FAIL IS TO
STOP
KEEP GOING...

DON'T LET FEELINGS
RUN THE SHOW

Imagine you feel excited to do or start something and then partway in you lose that excitement?
You lose the inspiration? It starts to get hard and you think...
Maybe I shouldn't be doing this.
Maybe God wants me to do something else.

Because you are reading this book, I know you have felt like this in the past.

I've felt that way. A LOT.
I've changed directions. A LOT.
And it was a mistake.

When I first started offering group programs, I had a hard time selling. It was so uncomfortable. I couldn't find my people. I couldn't describe what I did in a way people understood. After a bunch of NOes, I told myself, *Maybe I'm not supposed to help people in this way. Maybe I'm supposed to do something else.*

But that was a lie.

My lack of success wasn't a sign to quit. It was a sign that I sucked at sales, a sign that I didn't know my messaging. Because I was so uncomfortable making an offer, I came across as weird. I was scared. And I was looking for a way out.

There is a moment, a time when you feel inspiration, you feel Spirit, you feel the calling and you are 100% in.

And then after that moment, life happens and your mind starts to come up with all these reasons why it won't work. You don't have the money or the time. You can't figure it out. You can't see the full path.

Or obstacles come up. Maybe you have two people at your workshop or no one. Maybe no one is buying your artwork or healing sessions. Maybe you can't seem to figure out the email system or you can't figure out the end of your book.

And you stop,
And think. This is TOO hard.
If I was meant to do this, it should be easy, right?

Wrong.

Where did you get that idea?
The idea that doing your soul work, your creative calling should be easy all the time.

There are times this work feels amazing. I feel guided. I feel free. There are times I create with ease and connect to the creative momentum and flow.

Other times I question what I'm doing, especially when I'm learning a new task and I am falling on my face over and over again. Sometimes our work is big and it brings up all our fears and doubts and voices.

Look at leaders...

Martin Luther King
Gandhi
Mother Teresa
Dalai Lama
Oprah
Brené Brown

Do you think what they did or do was always EASY?

When you are bringing light and love into this world, when you are taking a stand for creativity or empowerment or speaking truth, STUFF will come up.

You must grow into who you need to be in order to do your work.
You're gonna have to learn new skills,
Grow a thicker skin,
Open your heart more than you ever have before.
And that can feel hard.
That can feel scary.
It can feel like an initiation... because it is.
An initiation into a deeper level of your calling.

So next time you tell yourself, "This is too hard." Ask yourself, "Is this really too hard, or is this my next initiation?"

REPETITION IS AN OPPORTUNITY FOR SELF-REFLECTION

I first heard that from Debbie Rosas, co-founder of The Nia Technique.

I've always thought of repetition as boring. I have been the girl to go to the next thing... Move on when things get stale. It was my way of keeping things exciting, not getting bored, of not having to think too much. Repetition was boring, lifeless...

My way to keep it fresh when I was younger... Travel. After my mother died, I left for a year to study abroad in Finland. Three years later, I was in Japan. Two years after that, I was in Mexico. And months after that, in Spain. Each time, a new adventure. I learned a new language, saw different sites, met new people. I loved it.

It was also my crutch. I didn't take time to slow down. When I did, I felt like I needed to add something else in. It was my way of not coping.

When Tony, my now-husband, then-boyfriend, broke up with me, my first instinct was to go to another country. A little extreme, but normal for me. It would be a way I would forget my pain and throw myself into something else. It would be an adventure and keep my mind off my pain. I decided instead to stay and sit in the pain. It hurt. But in that space of self-reflection, I was able to see what I wanted to change and changed it.

Instead of ignoring the fact we had two different religions, I really thought about it, tuned in to my heart, and made a decision that would work for him and me as well as our future kids. If I had instead zipped off to Japan, I would have missed the space for deep reflection. I wouldn't have had the time. And, I would not be married to my love.

I see this many times when I'm creating. I have points in my painting where I think, gosh it would be so much easier to start a new painting instead of sticking with this one. I like the beginning stages of the painting when it's just color and design and things are really rough, but when it gets to the point of putting in fine details and tending to my painting, meditating with her, and finishing her up, this is where I want to start something new. And many times I do. I have probably 15 paintings that are not finished.

The way you are in one area reflects the other areas of your life.

In relationships -- when things feel repetitive with your partner -- instead of thinking something is wrong, what, if instead you saw the chance for more intimacy?

In your workouts -- when things feel boring -- instead of thinking you need to find the next exciting thing, what if instead you saw the chance to connect to your body differently?

If you are going from thing to thing to thing, or if things are always fresh and new, you stay at the surface. You aren't able to dig deep, to find another layer of intimacy.

When you're feeling bored ask yourself:

How can I make changes here?
How can I pay attention to what's different?
How can I find what's new?
Why am I bored? What's really going on here?

In order to complete what you start, you must break this pattern. What if instead of doing something else new, you do what you have been doing, again and again, getting better and better and better at it. In the repetition, you can see what needs to change, what to make better. By doing this over and over again, you're able to help and serve deeper. Yes, your Muse sometimes may get pissed because she's ready to do the next thing already, but remember repetition is an opportunity for self-reflection.

FINISH STRONG

I've always been a strong starter,
crummy finisher.
I would Start out pumped up, excited.
Full of possibilities and ideas.

Then reality would set in.
Life in its busyness would show up,
Or I'd get bored,
Or I'd find something else WAY more exciting.

I decided to practice finishing.
To pace myself.
To celebrate commitment.

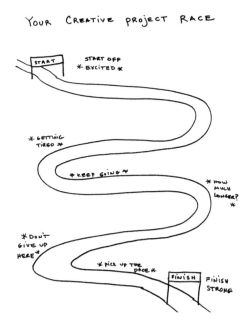

YOUR CREATIVE PROJECT RACE

START OFF * EXCITED *

START

* GETTING TIRED *

* KEEP GOING *

* HOW MUCH LONGER? *

* DON'T GIVE UP HERE *

* PICK UP THE PACE *

FINISH FINISH STRONG

I started practicing this commitment with everything...
With my creative projects,
With my workouts,
With my laundry.

I started training for a half marathon in order to practice finishing strong. Every run I'd notice when I wanted to give up and tell myself,
I finish what I start.
When I didn't want to finish writing a blog post, I'd tell myself,
I finish what I start.

While painting the edges of my painting, I'd tell myself,
I finish what I start.

After finishing what I started over and over again, I decided to do more than finish, but to finish STRONG.
To sprint the last bit of my run,
To put my full attention and love on my projects as I wrapped them up.

I ran my half marathon with my husband Tony. It was the last mile and I had hit my wall earlier. It was all I could do to keep my feet moving, one in front of another. But my husband kept me focused, just another bend, just a little longer. Finally, I saw the finish line and in that moment I knew I wanted to finish strong. I knew I had something left in the tank. I pushed it. I ran across that finish line and finished strong.

There's no better feeling.

What does finishing strong look like with your project?

. . . .

. . . .

. . . .

. . . .

. . . .

. . . .

. . . .

UNFINISHED PROJECTS

Here's how to focus and manage your creative project to completion:

First, choose what's most important to you right now, prioritize. Whatever I'm working on in my business, I have one priority. I'm not doing multiple things at the same time. I would not do an art show and plan a retreat at the same time. I've got one focus that I'm working on. Focus and prioritize. Some of that can shift when you have a team (if you're running a business) but we still have one main project.

Second, make it doable.
Set expectations that are realistic. Don't decide to do your first workshop ever and say you're gonna have 20 people and make tons of money. Set an expectation that feels good. With one of my clients, our expectation was just to do a workshop as our goal. It was her first workshop ever. Set an expectation that feels good for you because often times you are let down by your expectations.

Third, break it down.
Bite-sized pieces, small steps, things that are scary but not too scary. Break it down so it's so small you feel you can do it.

BIRTHING REQUIRES SOME PUSHING

Birthing a new project or mission or vision is work. Yes, there is joy and support but there are also times that feel hard.

When I'm painting, there are moments of total spirit connection... when things are flowing and it feels amazing and other moments I'm hating my painting and I'm wonder- ing how I'm going to pull it together... times I want to paint over it or put it in storage and start something new. But that is where the juice is.

When I had my first baby I had a hospital birth. I had a doula and for the most part, things went smoothly. My body knew what to do. I waited and waited to dilate fully so I could push. I remember my doctor telling me, Okay Amber, it's time to push. I would take a deep breath and puuuusssssssshhhhhhhhhhhhh while my doctor and all my support (Tony, Mom, Dad, and doula) would count to ten with me. I'd take a little break and then my doctor would watch the monitor to tell when another contraction was coming and tell me it was time to push again. It was hard but after 20 minutes, I pushed my baby out.

My second baby was a home birth. I had a midwife and things went very differently. My body still knew what to do but my midwife didn't tell me when it was time to push. She said I'd know when the time was right. Boy did I!

When it was time I couldn't do anything but push. My body took over. There was no counting to 10. I just rode the wave of my contractions.

This made me think of how it is when we birth projects or paintings or businesses. Sometimes we may listen to those who tell us it is time to push... and we do. And it is hard. It makes sense. We might be dilated (or ready to go) so we push. And projects are born. Sometimes projects are like my second birth. There isn't anything you can do but go along for the ride.

My point is, both births were hard. There was pushing involved. Grunt. Labor. Both times I decided I had changed my mind and no longer wanted to have a baby. It felt too hard... and yet that was right before the push. Right before they were born. Both were births.

So if you have hit the rough part, the pushing part, and you are tired and are thinking... maybe this isn't what you are meant to do, remember, there is pushing required for birthing creative babies too.

And you are right there.

MUSE TWEAKING

There may be a time when you need to adjust,
Your thinking,
Your schedule,
Your timeline.

Let go of rigidity in order to keep moving.

There's something inside that likes things to be tidy,
To be planned and controlled,
But creativity is like fire.
She's uncontrollable and sometimes the Muse must have her way.
And her way might not be yours.

So allow her some space.
Allow her to tweak what isn't working,
To give you her downloads,
Whenever and however they come.

She's so much happier when she's allowed freedom.

When things start to grind to a standstill and you're locked in,
It's time to move some blocks,
To get things rolling again.

It's time for some Muse Tweaking. Ready?

Here's what you do:
Put the pen in your Muse's hand.
Ask her to let you know what needs tweaking.
Ask her what she recommends.
Let the pen go.
Read it.
Then do what she says.

WRITE YOUR MUSE LETTER...

Dear BeLOVED,

Love,

Your Muse

RECOMMITTING

Feeling tired or bored?
Want to quit?

Time to recommit.

Recommitting is giving yourself a pep talk after you've fallen down again. You're either going to convince yourself to stop or keep going. In order to FINISH your creative work, you have to get good at talking yourself back into finishing.

I've been together with my husband Tony for 20 years.
I've had plenty of pep talks.
Every. Day.
Choosing, again and again, to be together, to do what it takes to make our marriage great.

When I'm mad and want to not talk to him, I get to choose to share how I'm feeling and REcommit.

When we lost two homes to foreclosure and we were stressed about money, I got to REcommit.

When I wanted to have another baby and he didn't, it was a choice to REcommit.

It's the same with your creative project.
There are days you'll be mad at your project,
Days you will feel like nothing is working,
Days you will want to start something new.
Time to REcommit.

I recommit by thinking of how AMAZING it will feel to be done. The people who will read my book or see my painting or wear my scarf.

FOCUS

List out all the things you're currently focused on
(people, projects, things, etc.)

. . . .

. . . .

. . . .

. . . .

. . . .

. . . .

. . . .

. . . .

. . . .

. . . .

. . . .

. . . .

WOW! You've got lots on your mind, Sister

PRIORITY

What do you want your focus to be?

. . . .

. . . .

. . . .

. . . .

What is out of order/feels out of balance for you?

. . . .

. . . .

. . . .

. . . .

What gets in the way of focusing on that?

. . . .

. . . .

. . . .

. . . .

COST + REWARD

How are you rewarded, what's the benefit of not focusing on this?

. . . .

. . . .

. . . .

. . . .

What's the **cost** of not focusing?

. . . .

. . . .

. . . .

. . . .

How can you focus on this **today**?

. . . .

. . . .

. . . .

. . . .

Let's do this!!

DECLARATION

i _____ AM

FOCUSING ON _____

SO THAT _____

_____

SPIRIT HAS PUT THIS IN
MY HEART. i AM CHOOSING
TO FOCUS + FOLLOW THROUGH.

i COMPLETE WHAT i START

_____   _____
SIGNATURE   DATE

MIND THE GAIN, NOT THE GAP

Years ago I put together a creativity workshop and no one attended. No one.

I was feeling low and my coach told me to "mind the GAIN, not the GAP."
To look at what was working WELL instead of what wasn't working well.

My GAIN...
I put together a workshop last minute

My GAP...
Marketing

Just that tweak, minding the GAIN and not the GAP kept me going instead of quitting. It helped me look at the pieces that weren't working in relation to all the movement I HAD made.

Minding the GAIN keeps you focused on moving and forward progress. The GAP is about what isn't working. The GAP is where the critic likes to live and she is all about getting you to STOP your creativity.

So Mind the GAIN, not the GAP.

On the next page, write YOUR GAINS. What have you learned? What's working well?

Then write the GAP. Keep your focus on the GAINS to keep you moving.

· ·
· ·
· ·
· ·
· ·
· ·
· ·
· ·
· ·
· ·
· ·
· ·
· ·
· ·

AWESOME LIST

One of the biggest things that will stop you from completing (or even starting) your creative work is the CRITIC. Read more about her on page 236 to get to know yours well.

In order to combat that voice that tells you that you're not doing good enough, you must put in another voice.

One that knows how amazing you are,
Who knows what you've done,
Who knows how capable and committed you are.

The way we do that is by coming up with our AWESOME LIST. AN AWESOME LIST is a list of things to show yourself you're awesome when you don't necessarily feel awesome.

This awesome list is to remind you of your capabilities when that other voice takes over.

Your list can include...
I am a good listener.
I am a present mom.
I create beauty around me.

Your list can also be about what you've done.
For example... I was Betty Body, the lead in my fourth-grade school play. I traveled through Japan on my bike. I danced on the Merrie Monarch Stage (Olympics of Hula).

Your turn.

Afterward, when you start doubting yourself, take yourself back to a time you accomplished something amazing. Remember how you were, how you acted. How you felt. You've already done it. You know how. Now you just get to do it again.

AWESOME LIST

1. . . . .

2. . . . .

3. . . . .

4. . . . .

5. . . . .

6. . . . .

7. . . . .

8. . . . .

9. . . . .

10. . . . .

11. . . . .

12. . . . .

13. . . . .

14. . . . .

15. . . . .

AWESOME LIST continued...

16. . . . .

17. . . . .

18. . . . .

19. . . . .

20. . . . .

21. . . . .

22. . . . .

23. . . . .

24. . . . .

25. . . . .

26. . . . .

27. . . . .

28. . . . .

29. . . . .

30. . . . .

AWESOME LIST continued...

31. . . . .

32. . . . .

33. . . . .

34. . . . .

35. . . . .

36. . . . .

37. . . . .

38. . . . .

39. . . . .

40. . . . .

41. . . . .

42. . . . .

43. . . . .

44. . . . .

45. . . . .

Keep going!

DONE IS BETTER THAN PERFECT

It's better to get things done than to have everything be perfect... because perfect never gets done. Perfectionism is crippling. I know this beastie lives in you and comes out every now and again.

The thing is, perfectionism doesn't show up all the time... like when you're doing laundry. It's not like you spend hours folding your laundry until it's just right. She shows up when you're worried about what other people will think.

She showed up before I read my first poem,
Hung my first painting,
Taught my first dance class,
Interviewed my first expert,
Published my first blogpost...

Perfection also showed up when I invested with my first business coach and took my first painting course... waiting for the right time (a.k.a. perfect time).

This is what I realized: There is no perfect time.

I get it. I used to say I need to pray about something or that when things are meant to be, it will line up, but the reality is, I was just scared. I didn't trust myself to make a decision so I would wait for 'signs.'

So this is my encouragement to you... If you are waiting for the right (a.k.a. perfect) time or want to make sure things are perfect before launching/sharing/submitting/trying/doing what you love, please just remember, better done than perfect.
What is perfectionism stopping you from doing?

ELIZABETH'S STORY (FOCUS)

Elizabeth was a manager at her family-run chocolate store. During the day she managed the store, employees, training, even early morning appearances on the local news. What she really wanted to do was create.

When we first started working together, she had two places of focus. She is a Potter and does pottery. She wanted to get her work in more galleries. She also wanted to teach workshops. When we first started working together we tapped into the Warrior and created a plan and focused on getting her work into galleries. We immediately got her in and she was selling her work within the first two months.

Then we focused on putting together a workshop. First, we set expectations, the expectation to do the workshop and practice leading. Next, we broke it down into small things for her to work on. The first, to fill the workshop. We came up with a plan for a way for her to do that. After that, I got a message from her a couple of weeks before the workshop was supposed to go live. I emailed her, asking how it was going, and hadn't heard anything back.

She finally shared, "I have zero people signed up for the workshop and I'm feeling like I should do a woman circle instead."

When I talked to her I found out she'd only done part of our plan to fill the program... she'd printed up flyers and hung them which was a stretch for her, posted on Facebook, and that was it.

I see this with creative business people, all the time. They want to make money and think just by putting up a website, or a flyer, boom the people are gonna come. That doesn't happen. You have to focus. You have to tap into your Queen.

One of the things Elizabeth and I had talked about was for her to call people up and invite them. I asked her, Who do you know? She told me she'd already come up with a list of people to call. I told her, I'm gonna hang up the phone right now. Call me back when you've made your first call.

She called me back five minutes later excited. Her energy had shifted. She could see the bigger vision of what she was creating again and it got her moving. It wasn't that she got a yes for her workshop. (The person actually wasn't able to come to the workshop), but she felt much less scared. She had faced it. She'd faced the fear. In the end, she sold the workshop out and decided to do another workshop the following month. She was thrilled because her expectations were to simply do it. Super celebration mode. She actually faced the stuff that was hard for her, focusing through to the end.

Since Elizabeth learned the power of focus and how to use her creative archetypes, she has left the chocolate store and is running her own online creativity company helping thousands of women around the world.

Focus is the magic fuel to find momentum.

SAGE'S STORY (FOCUS)

Sage was a writer. She had published several books and for almost 15 years ran a small publishing company alongside her husband Bradley. When we first met, she wanted to grow her business and help more writers by coaching them to finish their books. She focused on the first step, growing an audience of writers and her business grew.

While on a retreat together here in Hawaii, we got a call. Bradley had unexpectedly died in the middle of the night.

Sage was overwhelmed. She was in her early 40s and had four children at home and didn't know what life would look like now. So she focused on one thing in front of her at a time, arrangements for Bradley, organizing all the backend, taking care of the kids. She told me, "This taught me not to wait. Life is now."

She focused on building her writing coaching practice and within a year had doubled the income she and Bradly had made before. All while finishing the third book in a trilogy. She focused on what was most important and did it. Last year she met up with me again for another retreat in Hawaii. This time she brought all her kids.

She said the most fulfilling thing was seeing her kids so excited to see what's possible when you focus. She lived the energy of Queen, creating what she wanted in spite of the circumstances.

CELEBRATION

Most times when you finish up, you're ready for the next thing. Next. Next. Next.

But CELEBRATION is what brings creative momentum into your next project. It sources the energy from your previous project and brings it forward.

If you don't take the time to celebrate, you'll eventually burn out. You've gotta refuel. This is the fueling station.

I didn't know how to celebrate. My husband Tony taught me how. He celebrates everything.

He celebrates when he gets NOs after a proposal.
He celebrates when he tries something new (even if he fails).
He celebrates when a new client signs up.

When I won my first juried art show, I went to the reception, and afterward, when I got in the car to go home, he said, "So where are we going to celebrate?" I thought we already had, but no. We had to celebrate with intention. So we did.

He took me out to dinner.

Celebration, gratitude.
They go hand in hand.

So now we get to celebrate.

What are you celebrating? (any small or large thing that you've changed for the better, improved, made progress on, finished, etc)...

So now we get to plan your celebration(s)...
What are you going to do to celebrate?

CHAPTER 7

Top Creativity Blocks
+ THE PATH FORWARD

- WILL THEY JUDGE ME?
- AM I READY?
- IS IT GOOD ENOUGH?
- WHAT IF I MAKE THE WRONG DECISION?
- I DON'T WANT TO BE UNCOMFORTABLE
- I HAVE TO DO ALL OR NOTHING
- I NEED TO WAIT FOR INSPIRATION
- I NEED TO BE REALISTIC
- I NEED TO FIND THE TIME
- I'M WAITING FOR THE RIGHT TIME
- I NEED TO WAIT UNTIL EVERYTHING CALMS DOWN (*OVERWHELM*)
- I CAN'T DECIDE (*UNCLEAR/NOT SURE*)
- WHO AM I? (*CRITIC*)
- I SHOULD ALREADY KNOW THIS
- I DON'T THINK I CAN
- SHE'S SO MUCH BETTER THAN ME (*COMPARISON*)
- I'M FEELING TOO MUCH PRESSURE
- I NEVER DO WHAT I SAY I'M GOING TO DO. WHY TRY?

WILL THEY JUDGE ME?
NOT CARING CAN BE
A GOOD THING

Remember how you used to be as a kid?
Before you were told how you should think or act or speak.
Before you were told how to walk or dance or dress.
Before you were told your drawing wasn't good, your voice wasn't in tune, being a writer wasn't a real job.
Before you listened to it.
I remember.

"You were born an original. Don't die a copy." - John Mason

I took my youngest son Bodhi, bowling with four of his friends for his 10th birthday party. Five 10-year-old boys and me. On the way down to the bowling alley, driving in the minivan, we were listening to songs on the radio. One came on and all five of them belted out the song lyrics. It was loud, out of tune, and totally AWESOME.

No fear. No embarrassment. No hiding or shrinking. Full blast.

As I was watching them through my rearview mirror I thought... THIS, this is what gets trained out of us, this originality, this freedom.

What was it like when you didn't care about what people thought?

UNLEASHED TIP

Close your eyes and remember you when you were seven years old. What does she want you to do or say? Choose one of her recommendations today and do it.

AM I READY?
BE READY-ISH

I do live retreats once a year. One hundred women fly in from
all over the world. These retreats almost never happened.

Years ago I wanted things to be just right.
I needed to be certified,
Have more experience.
I needed to feel ready.
But I never did feel ready.
Luckily, I decided instead to go with feeling ready-ish.

Ready-ish means you let go of perfection.
Of needing it to be right.
Of needing it to flow smoothly.
Of needing people to like you,
Or think you're awesome,
Your artwork and writing, unique and well-received.

Ready-ish is about putting together what you can to the best
of your ability and moving forward anyway, knowing it might
be a bit messy in the process.

Here's the thing...
Perfection doesn't exist.

There are always hiccups,
Things that go wrong.
A sandstorm on the beach, when you're meant to lead an ocean
ritual,
You forget to hit save and lose a chapter of your book,
Your music shuts off in the middle of dance class,
Your wet painting falls over leaving a smudge right through the
middle of the canvas.

What have you been holding back on, waiting for it to be just right? Waiting for it to be perfect?

What do you have to do to let yourself and your project be ready-ish?

UNLEASHED TIP

Instead of thinking of all the reasons something isn't ready.
Make a list of all the reasons it IS.

IS IT GOOD ENOUGH?
THE EXPECTATION CYCLE

One of the biggest things I see that stops women from doing what they REALLY want is their expectations of how they think it should be. Like...

You start painting and expect your work to look beautiful, or
You start writing your book and expect it to flow, or
You want to teach a workshop for the first time and you expect to sell out.

Here's the thing: You can't succeed if you set your beginning expectations on someone else's ending results.

The Expectation Cycle looks like this...

You have an expectation,
Don't get the results you expect,
Feel bad,
Then quit.

What if you just got off that cycle so you don't give up or move on?

Where do you have expectations that are holding you back?

Where are you holding yourself to a standard you don't have the experience yet to meet?

UNLEASHED TIP

Write down the expectations keeping you from creating.
Where do those expectations come from?
Who or what are you comparing yourself to?

WHAT IF I MAKE THE "WRONG" DECISION: THE "RIGHT" DECISION

How do you know if you're making the right decision?

For most of my life, when it was time to make a big decision, I'd go back and forth, weighing the options. Could I do it? Would I be successful? What was the "right" choice? I even had trouble making decisions about what to eat for dinner or what to wear. (I'm a Libra, you know.)

Not making decisions uses up A LOT of time and energy. Time thinking, going back and forth in indecision.

I see it with women who want to create and make a difference. They spend too long deciding...
Where to hold the workshop.
How much to charge for the painting.
What to call the book.
What font to use on their cards.

They are waiting for the clouds to part and angels to sing as a sign.

Clarity rarely comes that way.

Most times your soul knows. You feel it. It's exciting and expansive, then...
You talk yourself out of it.

You know what you really want, but you don't trust yourself.

Maybe you've made "bad" decisions in the past,

Or have a history of not doing what you say you're going to do.

Maybe it feels safer to sit in indecision and just think about "it." Going back and forth. Weighing the options. Looking at what makes sense.
But we're not letting any more weeks or months or years pass in the thinking.

What if there isn't a right decision?
What if you took the pressure off and tried a decision on?

UNLEASHED TIP

Clarity comes when you're in action, not thinking. Take one small action even if you're not sure what to do. By doing the action, you'll get clear one way or another. What's the one small action you are willing to take right now?

. . . .

. . . .

. . . .

. . . .

. . . .

. . . .

. . . .

I DON'T WANT TO BE UNCOMFORTABLE: MOVE THE PAIN

There are things that pop up that are painful and uncomfortable. You might be fighting with a friend, caretaking your parents, battling with your kids, feeling ignored by your partner. You may feel lost and wonder about your purpose or be beating yourself up about not finishing your book or another creative project.

When it gets painful, what do you do?
I either stuff it or move it.
When I stuff it, I distract myself with social media, binge eating, drinking, pulling the covers over my head, and sleeping.

Eventually, the pain needs to move. One of my favorite ways to move it is through ART.

If you are in your pain right now, beating yourself up or feeling low, I want you to know, I know that hurt. I'm encouraging you to embrace ALL of you.

Move your pain your way... Dance it, paint it, pray it, sing it.
What ways do you normally distract yourself from pain?
What ways do you move your pain?

UNLEASHED TIP

Write your intention on your page or canvas.
Write/paint your pain.
Let it flowwwww out until you feel a shift...
Be kind to yourself. You've done beautiful work, honey.

Creativity UNLEASHED

SHARE ALL OF YOU

Sometimes I speak on stage and share my story. It would be
easy to talk about the successes and the times I look good... like
Having grown a $1.5 million creative business, or
Selling tens of thousands of dollars of artwork,
Taking my kids to Disneyland,
Traveling to France with my sister or England with my husband,
Because my creative business gave me the freedom to do so.

Those things are true. But they don't create connections.

You may think...
I could never do that, or
She's bragging, or...
Why are you telling me this, or
I don't want to hear that.
By sharing ONLY one piece, there isn't connection.
The connection is in ALL of it.

In order to have my success, I've gone through hard times.

When I started, I had no money.
Our first home had been foreclosed on.
Our second home was getting foreclosed on.
We had to close down our business and I had to negotiate
with creditors.
We went on assistance for food and medical.
I had to dig through my son's piggy bank for 97 cents so I could
buy a package of mac n cheese for dinner.

It is embarrassing to write, but this is ALL of it.

If you are missing connection with your art and writing, it's time
to share ALL of it

UNLEASHED TIP

Go back to your work and ask yourself, what do I NOT want to do to this painting? What feels risky? What do I NOT want people to know that I need to add into my writing? How can I bring ALL of me to my creation?

WHEN YOU FEEL LIKE STOPPING

What's getting loosened up for you?
What expansion is happening?
Where is your intuition leading you to something bigger, something greater?

Sometimes when you're feeling the calling, it feels like an uncomfortable stretch. And it just seems like such a better idea to not try, not put yourself out there, not do it.
Here are three things to do when you feel like stopping:

BREATHE
Three breaths. One to let go of the past, one to let go of the future, and one to inhale and smell THIS moment. By getting present, you have more tools available to you. You become more yourself. Less worried, stressed, thinking. More here, now. There's lots of science to back this up.

CREATE
Sometimes when you're feeling a lot, you need to release it, like a pressure valve. Creativity releases. So whether you are painting, writing, art-journaling, doodling, carving, knitting, dancing, whatever... release. Let it go. Let it out.

CONNECT
The biggest mistake I see when women feel overwhelmed or shaken up is to pull back. You try to make your world more manageable. Be more IN control. Cutting things out instead of finding a way through. When you feel the urge to pull back, to put the painting aside, to scratch the song, to put the manuscript away, instead ask yourself, WHO do I need to connect with?

Connection will help you see possibilities you may have missed.

Here's to throwing your arms open when you feel like stopping. Congrats. It's a sign you're on the creative path.

I HAVE TO DO ALL OR NOTHING: OR DO YOU?

You know that all or nothing thing that happens?

You don't exercise at all, then decide to work out seven days a week. You decide to put your artwork out there then decide to finish 10 paintings. You start leading workshops then decide to do three back to back. You decide you want to put together a website and that means 10 webpages with your offerings, bio, artwork, workshops, a blog...

It's all or nothing.

You're inspired and your eyeballs are bigger than the plate in front of you. And you decide you can do it all.

But you can't.

I used to do this... 0 to 60mph. Then crash. What if you ease in? Pace yourself? Rest?

Here's the thing with all or nothing... most times it just leads to giving up. It leads to unfinished projects because you bite off more than you can chew then beat yourself up for not chewing all of it.

UNLEASHED TIP

Here's how to keep yourself out of all or nothing...
Whenever you start something new, have three goals...

An I-did-it goal (woohooo) ·
An I-did-pretty-good goal, and ·
An I'm-a-superstar goal ·

This keeps you out of the all or nothing mindset and allows
you to see more options. It keeps you from giving up or
breaking down when you can't do it all.

So if you're finding yourself in ALL OR NOTHING, break it
down. Pace yourself. Even something is better than nothing.

I NEED TO WAIT
FOR INSPIRATION

Do you ever feel you need to wait for the inspiration to come?
You need to wait until you're in the creative mood?

We've all been in moments where we feel the creative flow.
It feels amazing when things are coming through so easily. It's
no wonder we want it to feel that way all the time when we are
creating. But, we don't always feel the creative flow, do we?

Think of your creativity as a relationship.
You get to show up for it whether you feel like it or not.

Sometimes the best ideas come up when you're in creative
flow and inspired in the moment. Other times that inspiration

comes from you just starting. Just the act of getting moving or doing will open up the gates to what is good.

Creativity isn't a passive act.
It isn't something that magically happens sometimes.
It is co-creating with spirit.
It is you showing up and choosing to allow inspiration.
It is you saying, I am willing to be here waiting for whatever happens.

This is your creative act of faith.

UNLEASHED TIP

When you don't feel like creating, set the timer for 15 minutes and just create. Do not pay attention to whether you think it is good or not good. Just write, paint, dance, draw. 15 minutes of faith. Watch what happens.

I NEED TO BE REALISTIC-
OR DO I?

Do you believe it's important to be realistic? Have you had your dreams squashed by a realist? No fun. I learned my lesson the hard way (and it's not the way you're thinking).

My husband Tony and I were out on the town for a date. This was years ago, early in our marriage. This was our time to connect as we both were working 60-70+ hours a week. Our evening was going well. He was telling me about an idea he had to open another business.

I told him the reasons why I thought it was a bad idea. I talked about finances and risk and his skill set. I watched the sparkle leave his eyes and saw his hurt. I watched his heart close down. He leaned over and said, "All I wanted was for you to be excited for me and believe in me."

I thought I WAS being supportive. I told him so. I said, "Babe, I'm just being realistic." He said, "No, you're not. You're being pessimistic."

And looking at him I realized, what I called realistic was pessimistic. It is socially accepted disbelief.

I thought about all the times I had decided to be realistic and I asked myself, "What good did it do to be realistic?" Is being realistic an excuse to be a downer? Is being realistic a way to keep people from getting too excited, to keep them from getting their hopes up? Is it a way for me to feel better about myself, keeping someone at my level? Keeping myself small?

I grew up in a family where realistic was celebrated. It meant having a good head on your shoulders, seeing things as they were. It was considered intelligent and thoughtful. That night I decided to end that lineage.

Being realistic is about keeping people small. Keeping them in a box. Maybe keeping you in a box?

It has to do with the belief of whoever is speaking about being realistic. When someone has a big vision, bringing realism to it is a way to poke holes in it.

Many people have told me my vision wasn't realistic...
That artists don't make good money,
That I need _____ (fill in the blank) certificate to teach,
That running a business takes a lot of time.

And yet... I have worked with over 80,000 women online using art and creativity making great money doing what I love part-time. As I write this, I'm now working a 20-hour work week.

People don't see how it can happen so they think it can't.

If you have a dream or vision and someone is telling you it's unrealistic, or the voice in your head tells you to be realistic... Remember anyone who did anything great, was first considered unrealistic. Gandhi, Martin Luther King Jr., Oprah, J.K. Rowling, Van Gogh, Ford, the first plus-sized models, the first women doctors...

If you consider yourself a realist, check yourself. Is it really helping? Or just helping you stay small? What if you let go of your lineage of being realistic and instead leave a LEGACY of dreams and vision?

What if you hang out with the dreamers and visionaries, those who believe in miracles and mystery?

What could be possible?

UNLEASHED TIP

Write one unrealistic thing you want to do and why it makes total sense to do it.

I NEED TO FIND THE TIME: NO TIME

How are you doing? Busy.

It's just normal conversation to say we're busy and we don't have the time to do what we want to do.
You have a creative calling and think, I'm gonna get to it when my kids leave or when I don't have to take care of my parents anymore or after summer break, or next year and you keep putting off what you wanna be doing, putting it off, putting it off, putting it off and then it just doesn't happen because you're not creating the time.

You're never gonna find the right time. "The right time" is a myth. Life is always coming up with new ways of needing you. You have to make the time.

I know right now you may be saying, "But Amber, You don't know my schedule. But, Amber you don't know my situation." I know life is full. I'm a mom. I have kids. I have a husband. I can't go away to go write somewhere at a retreat. I can't take hours at a time to paint. I have a business. I have employees. I volunteer at my kids' school. I dance hula. I'm running a half marathon. I work with private clients. I have group clients. I have tons on my plate and I'm still finding time every day to do creativity for me, even if it's just 15 minutes.

I've helped moms of young kids, women who are taking care of their elderly parents, who have a partner who's dying or they themselves are dying. Professionals who are working super long hours, entrepreneurs (who work all the time), retired people who have an abundance of time but no structure. All different people who need different schedules.

UNLEASHED TIP

There's a process that I created to help you take and create a personal creative practice. There are four pieces to it. This whole book is dedicated to it.

But here's a summary:

SCHEDULE
Look at frequency, timing, your energy, and the different times of a day. What works best for you?

PLAN FOR WHAT'S GOING TO TAKE YOU OUT
You already know what stops you or what has stopped you in the past from doing what you say you're going to do. Come up with a plan for life happening.

SET BOUNDARIES
You know when people ask you to do something and you have something scheduled, but you put yourself off in order to make people happy? That's boundaries (or lack of boundaries). Why are you saying yes to things that you really want to say no to? Find a compassionate way to say no, so you're not as worried about what people are gonna think when you tell them No.

SEEK OUT SUPPORT
You need buddies to keep you on your practice, to pick you up when you fall down. The buddy system is the way to go.

If you keep putting your practice at the bottom of the pile, you are telling yourself you, your art, or your work isn't important.

WAITING FOR THE RIGHT TIME: THERE IS NO RIGHT TIME

How do you make the time you have work for you? We all have the same 24 hours a day. We all have a limited amount of time before we leave this planet. How are you making your time work for you? How do you get the most out of it?

It was May 1991. I was in eighth grade, almost the end of the school year. I was in track. County finals were coming up. I trained for shot put. (Bet you wouldn't have guessed that.)

It was an ordinary day and my mom and dad wanted to get up early to go pick up their friends from the airport. I didn't want to go. It was dark. I was a typical 13-year-old. I just wanted to stay in bed and sleep. My brother and I climbed in the back of the Buick. Slept on the way down. We got to the airport and parked.

I'll never forget this moment. Mom and Dad turned around from the front seat and handed my brother and me gifts. My brother and I looked at each other a little confused and slowly unwrapped the tissue paper. We found two Mickey Mouse T-shirts. We were going to Disneyland!!!!

My parents explained they had packed everything and had made arrangements with our teachers at school. My track coach knew I was missing the county finals. All we needed to do was get on the plane to Disneyland.

At Disneyland, my mom and I decided to ride Space Mountain. If you haven't ridden it before, it's a roller coaster in the dark, lit only by black light. I get in the seat with my Mom. It's pitch black. We take off and my Mom starts laughing uncontrollably. I have no idea what's going on. She couldn't stop laughing.

Apparently, I had fallen asleep on a black light stamp the night before and that stamp was glowing all over my face. That moment with my mom belly laughing is one of the best memories I have with her.

That trip was also the last trip I ever took with my mom. She was diagnosed with cancer three months later and died six months after that.

Last April, I found myself sitting on the plane about to take off with my husband and kids. We were taking the kids to Disneyland and they had no idea.

For 10 years I tried to take the kids to Disneyland. Ten years. It was never the right time. Never had extra money. Other things were more important. Disneyland was a someday wish. Someday we'll have the time. Someday we'll have the money.

One year, I said, Enough! Life is now and thinking of mom, I thought, life isn't guaranteed. I booked the flight, hotel, and created the most magical experience for my family.

So there I was on a plane with Tony giggling and laughing. We weren't in a Buick. We were on a plane and the kids had no idea we were going to Disneyland.

When we arrived we decided to ride Splash Mountain. It's a giant log ride. You're gonna get wet. My oldest wanted to ride it. I bought a poncho, we braved the line, climbed the slippery wet steps into a log, and settled in, him sitting in front of me. And we were off.

As I rode the ride, I started crying. Holding my son, arms wrapped around him, I remembered hearing the same songs with my mom, her arms wrapped around me, feeling the excitement as we rode the log ride knowing we were about to go off the drop.

I thought of how she must have loved holding me and creating that moment together. Knowing I was about to become a teenager and our relationship would change forever. She had no idea it would be the last trip we'd take together. She was 41.

The average life expectancy of a woman in the United States is 78 years.

There are two ways of thinking:

Thinking you always have time, procrastinating, and at the end of the day, month, year not doing what you want to do because it's not the right time.

The other is creative, playful, passionate, wanting to live life now. Following your calling.

Not everyone says Yes when opportunity comes. But you are. Right now. Say Yes to your creative calling. It's time. Don't wait.

UNLEASHED TIP

Instead of waiting for the right time, say to yourself, Now is my time.

I NEED TO WAIT UNTIL EVERYTHING CALMS DOWN

WHERE ARE YOU OUT OF RHYTHM?

WHAT IS CALLING FOR BALANCE?

WHEN DO YOU TAKE TIME TO PAUSE?

Start – stop, start – stop, start – stop. You start to go, you get excited, then life shows up, something happens and you stop again to get things handled, waiting for it to calm down again. When life happens, how can you keep moving forward?

WHAT ARE YOU READY TO CHANGE?

You're gonna get sick, people will die, there will be relationship problems. There'll be stuff at work. There are always things that show up. So how can you continue to move through this? How can you continue to connect to your joy, to your fun, to your play, to your creativity when life is happening?

STRUCTURE.

For the creative, structure can seem blah. There's the whole, I'm a creative, I'm an artist, I am a free person. You love your freedom. By having structure, you will have more freedom.

UNLEASHED TIP

Where are you working too hard, not listening to your rhythm? That voice that says your creativity needs to wait is a LIAR.

I CAN'T DECIDE

Just choose.

I know it might be painful. It may feel like I'm asking you to choose your favorite kid at this point. But, just like kids, there are priorities. My oldest might need me more as he is going into Junior High and figuring out how to be himself and still be cool. Then in a couple of months my youngest might need me for help with his reading.

You can't do everything at the same time. Prioritize.

UNLEASHED TIP

This is the four-step process we take our clients through. If you have trouble deciding, let's do it together:

1. List all your choices here:

2. Which ones can you take off the list right away, you know they're definitely not at the top? Pare down to your top three.

. . . .

. . . .

. . . .

. . . .

3. Next ask yourself which one feels juiciest, lightest, most inspiring? Bring it down to two.

. . . .

. . . .

. . . .

. . . .

4. Once you get down to the final two, just choose one. Just choose. It really doesn't matter. You can go back and do that other thing after you've wrapped this one up. There is no right one. The fate of the world doesn't depend on this. You are held by something much bigger. Trust and choose.

WHO AM I?

Are you waiting to not feel fear to move forward?
Do you feel critical of your own work so you stop yourself?
Fear sounds like... My work isn't good enough, who's gonna want what I have?

Fear doesn't go away. Neither does that voice in your head. I wish I could wave some magical wand then you'd never criticize your work anymore. But I don't have that wand. I've talked to hundreds of other leaders, business coaches, artists, writers who'll tell you your critical voice doesn't go away. You learn to work with it.

Is that voice stopping you from trying? Maybe you're scared of what people think, you judge your work as not good enough, or tell yourself, "Who do you think you are?" You feel a fraud.

Or maybe you're comparing, "Their stuff is so much better. I don't have anything original, anything new to add."

Maybe your critical voice makes you feel guilty. "You're a bad Mom, wife, friend, etc. because you're spending time on your art instead of doing the dishes or making money. Art is a waste of time. It doesn't matter."

I also see this in women who want to make money. How you think determines how much you charge. Whether you feel you're worthy or not. Lots of creative women say, I just want to give my stuff away, I want everyone to be able to enjoy it. That is a beautiful give... your sacred creativity. Let me ask you, where's that coming from? Is it coming from thinking "No one's gonna pay full price for my stuff so I might as well give it away?"

What is the thinking stopping you from doing your creative work?

UNLEASHED TIP

Here's a method I use to work with my clients and their thoughts:

Look at your old story, the story that's shutting you down creatively ·
Create a new story ·
Learn what to do when the old one pops up ·

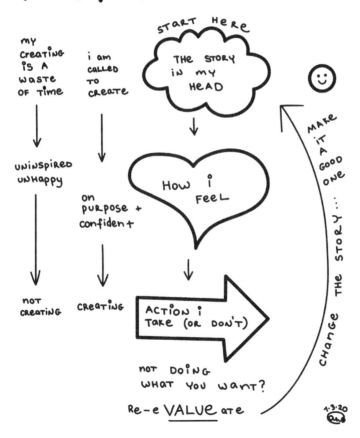

First let's look at the story that is currently running, the one that is keeping you stuck, the one that keeps you from starting or sabotages you along the way.

For example: No-one is ever going to read your book. You never went to writing school. You don't even have an original idea. What if it flops and it's terrible? You would have spent all that time on nothing.

Write your current story here:

. . . .

. . . .

. . . .

. . . .

. . . .

. . . .

. . . .

. . . .

. . . .

Next, we create a new story. Look at the old story. Think, that's an interesting story that's been running me for a long time. How can I change it?

For example: I have been writing all my life. Think of all the happy hours I'll get to spend writing, doing what I love whether other people love my book or not!

Write your new story here:

. . . .

. . . .

. . . .

. . . .

. . . .

. . . .

. . . .

. . . .

. . . .

. . . .

Last, we look at what to do when these old stories come up again, because they do. I've been doing my work for a loooooong time and I still have the story, I'm not good enough, my work's not good enough, What if they don't want what I'm offering? Those thoughts still pop up, but I have a way to manage them.

For example: Dance break, go for a walk, start writing, painting, call a friend who will remind me I'm amazing...

Make a list of things you can do when your old story pops up:

. . . .

. . . .

. . . .

. . . .

. . . .

. . . .

. . . .

. . . .

. . . .

WHAT KEEPS YOU FROM TAKING ACTION?

Imagine how you'd feel if you moved past that fear, if you took a step, if you were able to magically move that fear.

What could you do?

WHAT IS THE COST IF YOU DON'T TAKE ACTION?

WHEN YOU ARE STUCK HOW DO YOU GET IN ACTION AGAIN?

WHAT IS THE 1 ACTION YOU ARE CALLED TOWARD TODAY?

I SHOULD ALREADY KNOW THIS: DO IT ANYWAY

I want you to imagine us sitting down together. Me with my Earl Grey. You with something delicious.

I want to have a heart to heart, to listen to what's been going on with you lately. To hear you celebrate if you'd normally talk your awesomeness down. To hear you speak the truth if you normally fit into what others want or need. To give you a hug if you just need someone to be there while you let it go.

What's really stopping you?

I know what it's like to have a vision and a dream, to want something so bad, and yet you stop yourself again and again. I know what it's like to take those first steps forward, scared and unsure.

The first time I started painting, I was terrified. I remembered my grade school teacher telling me my art wasn't good and I still believed her 25 years later. But I wanted to paint. So I put my brush to canvas over and over again. I STILL hear the voices that tell me my art isn't good but I paint anyway.

It took me almost two years to start calling myself an artist in public. I practiced looking in the mirror and telling myself, "You are an artist!" Every time I said I was an artist, I felt a fraud. But I called myself one anyway. And it got more and more comfortable.

The first workshop I ran, I thought, Who am I to do this? There are so many better teachers out there, but I did it anyway.

That voice showed up,

When I published my first blog post.
When I did my first online retreat.
When I created an online class.
When I started doing sales.
When I started coaching clients.
When I hired a team.
When I hit six figures.
When I hit multiple six figures.

That voice never goes away.

I've learned not to let that voice lead me. It would be like letting
the smallest, most scared part of me take over. And what would
life be like with Her running the show?

You might know.
I did. For years.

I thought, I'd really like to _____. Then the voice
would pop up and remind me of all the reasons why I shouldn't.
And I'd go back to not doing anything.

That is until I found a way to change my thinking: mentors.
To get out of your head and your fear, you can't do it alone.

I know I've told you this before, but here's the thing...
Most of us believe we somehow should have this whole thing
figured out. We don't want to ask for help because we think we
should have the self-discipline to do it on our own.

We can't.

No one can.
Even if we KNOW something doesn't mean we DO it.

Need to call on support? Let's find your canoe crew on page 160.

I DON'T THINK I CAN:
WHATEVER YOU THINK IS TRUE

Years ago, my husband Tony and I coached with the owner of the Atlanta Hawks, Jesse Itzler, to stretch our minds more than they had been stretched before.

The idea was simple. He'd coach a group of us for 90 days on mindset and on the 90th day, we'd do an intense physical challenge, something that would test our willpower, our determination. And after completing that, everything else would seem easy.

The challenge?
Go up and down the hill to his backyard house 100 times. It's a grassy slope and slippery. It's 70 yards at a 30 degree angle, a total of 8.4 miles. Most of the hill is in full sun. He's had extreme athletes, NBA players, and Ironmen not finish.

It's called Hell on the Hill.

Out of the 34 of us who trained for the hill, 30 of us completed the whole thing. Jesse later said he thought maybe 50 percent of us would finish. His friends who were there to support thought, maybe 30 percent.

Here's one thing I learned on the hill: You can do more than you think.

When we started training with Jesse, he talked about under-indexing. At one point in his life, he wanted to run two miles at a 10-minute mile pace. He thought, if he could do that, it would be amazing. Shortly after that, he trained for a 100-mile race.

Same man. Same body. The difference? What he thought he was capable of.

"Whether you think you can, or you think you can't, you're right." Have you ever heard that quote? Henry Ford said it in 1949. Your mind will stop you from doing what you want. Your mind will tell you you're not able to do things when you still can.

So let's use the words from the *The Little Engine that Could*... I think I can, I think I can, I think I can...

> "Comparison is a thug that robs your joy. But it's been more than that - Comparison makes you a thug who beats down somebody - or your soul."
>
> – ANN VOSKAMP

MY CRITIC

Now draw YOUR CRITIC...

SHE'S BETTER THAN ME: INSPIRED COMPARISON

Everything is good. You're satisfied, dreaming, growing. Then you start doing it. Comparing.

Suddenly you're no longer unique and your paintings look like everyone else's.
Your writing is mediocre.
You could be doing way better as a mom,
Having hotter sex,
Making a bigger difference,
Making way more money,
Starting a podcast,
Yesterday.

You did it. You Compared your-self with others.

You see, when you compare, there's no more connection.
There is hierarchy.
Someone better, someone less.
Someone successful, someone not.
Someone's got it, someone doesn't.

You compare, and next thing you know, you're no longer content with what you have.

I do that as a mom. When I compare myself, I feel I should be doing SO much more. I should be making handmade cupcakes for my kids' birthdays and enrolling them in after school sports and paying for ukulele lessons. Or at least a tutor.

Or maybe, and this is hard to admit, you compare yourself to others and tell yourself, I'm better than them. I'm further along. I'm doing well. But when you're comparing and you come out ahead, you really don't. You just feel lonely.
The only thing separating you and holding you back are the thoughts in your head.

Here's a giant permission slip to pause the comparison, and to instead, choose connection.

So how do you change these thoughts from critical comparison to inspirational comparison?

8·15·20 YOU aLReaDY KNOW

Remember why you want to do what you want to do. (If you can't, go back to page 37.)

We all have different whys, reasons we do what we do, but the thing is, when you compare, you can't see that.

UNLEASHED TIP

What are the ways you compare yourself to others?

List them here:

Now, what ways can you be inspired instead?

I'M FEELING TOO MUCH PRESSURE: USE PRESSURE TO WORK FOR YOU

Ever feel pressure?
Like too much is coming all at once?
Like you have to take your foot off the gas in order to catch your breath?

Here's the deal, if you're making a difference in the world, you're gonna feel pressure. Welcome to the world of difference-makers, sister.

It's a privilege to feel pressure.

It means you are stretching. You are reaching beyond your comfort zone. You are making a difference. You are doing more than others around you.

So, if it's gonna happen anyway, How can you work WITH pressure?

1. **Change the way you're THINKING**

When I first started my work, I felt pressure writing a blog post. I'd spend a day or two crafting the perfect email. I felt pressure for it to be good. To be right.
Now, it takes me 30 minutes.

When I started leading workshops, I felt pressure holding space for four people. I wanted them to have a powerful experience. I wanted to make sure they all felt amazing at the end. Since then, I've led live retreats with 100. Four seems like a breeze.

The amount of work hasn't changed. I still write blog posts. I could still do an event for four. I just don't feel the pressure anymore. My mind isn't thinking it's hard.

2. USE pressure

Welcome her in.

Why fight pressure if it's coming anyway? Why not open your arms wide and welcome her like a friend? Celebrate. Throw a party.

Her appearance means you're doing something. You're stretching and growing. You're going through your own alchemical experience. Wonder what you're transforming into...

When you're feeling nervous or pressure or streeeeeeeeeeetched too thin, think of it as a pressure cooker. You're getting tender. You're softening in order to do your magical work in the world, in order to share your gifts.

So if you're feeling it, welcome to the privilege of pressure. Open wide. It means you're doing something.

And if pressure is feeling too much, let's go back and check your energy is good (page 88-89) and you've got a plan that isn't too full (page 116-121).

I NEVER DO WHAT I SAY I'M GOING TO DO. WHY TRY? A MESSAGE IF YOU'RE THINKING OF GIVING UP

If you're thinking of giving up on yourself, isn't it always too soon?

You're not giving yourself a chance.

The REAL thing that is stopping you from writing your book, running the workshop, sharing your art, starting the business, making an impact, is YOU.

The way you THINK.

Most people stop themselves from even TRYING. They stop before looking at possibility and so opportunities pass them by. And once those opportunities pass, they're gone.

I need you to hear me. THIS IS IMPORTANT.

Don't give up on yourself.
Don't convince yourself you're not worth it,
You have nothing to offer,
Others are better,
You can't make a difference.
Because you can.

The only thing that's gonna stop you is that voice in your head telling you it's better to not even try.

Imagine if EVERY WOMAN stopped the doubt, stopped listening to that voice that keeps her small, and instead just did it. Lived it. Owned it.

Imagine women unafraid to call the people and bring them together in... circles, workshops, and retreats.
Imagine women creating movements,
Imagine women sharing their art, healing, creating beauty, and making change through image,
Imagine women elders using their voices to speak up and share their teachings,
Imagine women having the courage to build the business and live the purpose they felt called towards.
Imagine women making money and then spending it in ways and in places they felt most called.
What could change?

I want to find out. I want to live in that world.
So let's make a pact sister:

Let's choose
To see,
To try,
To explore,
To vision,
To gather information,
To stay open,
To receive,
To not give up.

You ARE worth it. I know it.

UNLEASHED TIP

You know in the old days how when you misbehaved you had to write on the blackboard over and over again... "Telling a lie is wrong" or whatever they had you say? It's time to anchor in what you WANT.

I'm persistent.	I'm determined.	I finish what I start.	This is important.
I'm persistent.	I'm determined.	I finish what I start.	This is important.
I'm persistent.	I'm determined.	I finish what I start.	This is important.
I'm persistent.	I'm determined.	I finish what I start.	This is important.

Now your turn ...

LET GO OF RESISTANCE

Resistance to
Picking up the paintbrush,
Doing your daily meditation,
Calling women who need support,
Filling the last spots of a workshop,
Using social media,
Asking for help,
Saying yes,
Saying no.

Instead, listen to the calling that is asking you to just do it.
Let go of the resistance that tells you
It's hard or
Not worth it or
Not you or
Not good enough.

Being out of resistance allows you to make a bigger impact.
Less of your head telling you what's realistic, what's impossible,
and more of you just doing it.

What is your resistance?

UNLEASHED TIP

If your resistance looked like something, what would it look like?
I've given you a whole page to draw it...

YOUR RESISTANCE...

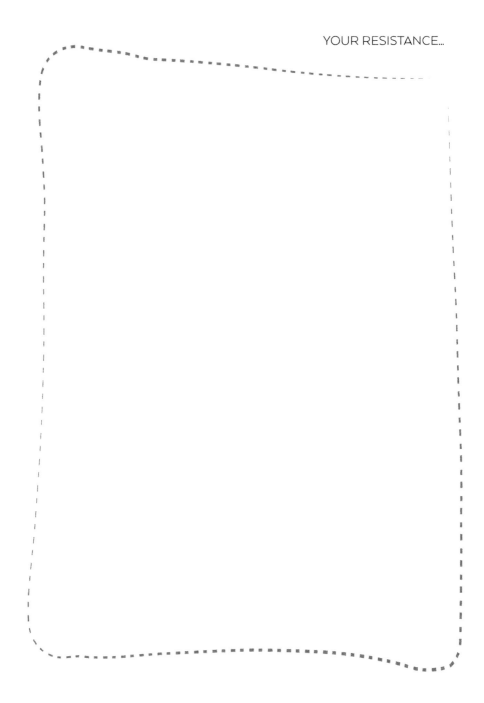

Now you've drawn it, make one small change to your image –
add a contrasting color or add a flower in there. Let's change it
visually to see what happens...

YOU'RE CREATED
TO CREATE

Your mind doesn't dwell in the same realm as miracles. If you
leave your decisions up to your mind, it's gonna talk you out of
everything that's new, that's different, that you haven't done
before. Everything.

The analytical mind looks at what's worked in the past. It's gonna
keep you there. But you can't grow or try new things there. You
have to tap into another side, spirit. Your connection to your
higher power, something greater than yourself.

We were created after Creator, Source, God, Goddess, Spirit,
or whatever that is for you. Our purpose is to create. We're
creating relationships, work, art, books, paintings, dance... There's
something you are meant to birth in this life. It's a drive for
every single one of us. We're created this way.

We're created to create.
If you don't make time to do that, you miss the Bliss.

So create.
Trust you have something to say,
You're worth the time,
You're worth the energy,
You're here to create.
You.

YOU ALREADY KNOW

I am writing to you from my heart.
A message to remind you what
You already know.

You have generations of knowing
Women who knew before you.
And women before them.

When you are wondering
What next?
You feel unclear,
The way is unsure, and
You don't know the next step,
Listen.

Listen deeply.
Take a breath.
Rest quietly.

You already know.

If you've gotten to the end of your creative cycle, guess what?
It's time to begin again. Let's move to your next creative calling.

Flip back to page 50 and choose another of your creative ideas.

Let's begin again.

Revisit for
CREATIVE
MOMENTUM

Every now and then we all feel like we need a refresher. If you are feeling like you need to tap back into creative momentum, a boost in your energy, a new structure or plan, support or the focus to finish, go directly to these sections for some inspiration.

Acknowledgements

To those who helped me unleash my creativity, Shiloh Sophia, Mama Caron McCloud, Sue Hoya Sellars, Lenore Thomas Straus, MUSEA: Intentional Creativity Foundation, and to Debbie Rosas, Carlos Rosas, and the Nia Technique.

To my writing mentor Mary MacDonald, who has encouraged me to write my book ever since she met me.

To my sister-friend Wendy Collier, who stood for me to put my writing first.

To my sister-hive Nikol, Jeniafer, Sacha, Anahita, Hemalayaa, Alexis, Deborah, SO much encouragement.

To our Unleashed Team, Elizabeth, Mirabai, Kate, Sam, Dominique, Christina, Lacey, you hold our ship together.

To Mom, Dad, Mom, Dad and Mom. I love you forever. You hold my possibilities.

To my family for loving me as I am.

To my vision keepers Lou Reed and Bay Le Quinn who kept me writing, who kept me from giving up.

To the Creativity Unleashed Book Team: Heather Doyle Fraser who helped organize my creative brain into a book, Vanessa Bell who made this book the most gorgeous ever, and to Jesse Sussman who has helped get this out to as many women as possible..

To our Mentorship Circle, Inner O sisters for honoring the sacred, creative path. To our Unleashers around the world, you inspired this work.

To my business coach Shanda Sumpter, who taught me to believe in myself and showed me creatives can make money in service and devotion.

Mahalo. Mahalo. Mahalo.

About the Author & Illustrator

Amber Kuileimailani Bonnici is Founder of Woman Unleashed®, a community dedicated to helping women connect to Spirit using creativity. She supports women through retreats, online membership, and mentorship programs.

Amber hosts the Woman Unleashed Online Retreat which has drawn over 85,000 women from over 128 countries since it first began. Her artwork has been featured in the U.N. Commission on the Status of Women and Women's Rights, An Artist's Perspective.

When she's not teaching or coaching, you'll find her on the Big Island of Hawai'i painting, writing, dancing hula or hanging with her husband and boys.

We want you to do more than read this book — We want you to create!

To help you do that, we've developed special resources and diving deeper training just for Creativity Unleashed sisters to get you started, keep you creating, get you going when you feel stuck, and give you the inspiration to finish up.

Go to **www.womanunleashed.com/book** to get started.

Printed in Great Britain
by Amazon

26553933R00153